Loganita Farm's

KITCHEN
GARDEN
COMPANION

Loganita Farm's

KITCHEN GARDEN COMPANION

Mary von Krusenstiern

with Anne Treat

Illustrations by Kristen den Hartog

Published in the United States by One Bird Press, LLC

Library of Congress Control Number: 2018956838

ISBN 978-1-7324229-2-6

Printed in the United States of America

For Steve McMinn, who created Loganita Farms as a family venture,
who believes in growing healthy food and in the goodness of work,
and who, when faced with the difficulties of this world,
likes to quote Voltaire: "Let us cultivate our garden."

CONTENTS

THE WILLOWS INN—SPECIAL REQUESTS

AN INDEX OF PESTS AND HOW TO MANAGE THEM

THE NITTY-GRITTY

FOREWORD

I love walking into our refrigerated room first thing in the morning, pulling out a large bin of vegetables, and expecting them to be cold but still feeling the sun's warmth on their skin.

For years, I have worked with Loganita garden and head farmer Mary von Krusenstiern, who grows unique and delicious produce exclusively for the Willows Inn. Mary is one of the most talented people I have ever met. Her farming knowledge is amazingly comprehensive, and she is unbelievably hardworking, passionate, and curious about plants. The plants must sense it as well, because they seem to sprout up around her as she walks down the rows. At some point most days she'll stop by the kitchen, son Trell in tow, checking in with the chefs about every detail of the menu and that day's harvest, constantly syncing her garden with our kitchen.

I know this book will excite any gardener or food lover, as it shares some of the discoveries that have made Loganita such an exceptional garden. Mary coaxes more from one acre of land than most do from five, and this book is full of techniques for how you, too, can get the most from every inch of your garden. Mary also makes some suggestions about the varietals that we love. When you buy fresh vegetables you're limited to standard varieties of crops, but when you grow your own, the world of specialty varieties opens up. There are countless plant varieties, hundreds of types of lettuces, beets, and potatoes.

Loganita garden would be a paradise for any chef. There is no describing the pleasure of watching the garden change through the seasons, or biting into a perfectly ripe vegetable just picked from the plant and imagining the perfect dish to make from it. I hope that this book inspires you to start your home garden as much as Mary and Loganita inspire me as a chef.

Blaine Wetzel

Feed your belly, heart, and mind

INTRODUCTION

Food tastes better when it's alive! Nothing compares to a carrot freshly pulled from the earth, a tomato that goes straight from the vine into your mouth, a salad of greens cut moments ago. There's magic in watching tiny seeds take root and grow; there's deep soul satisfaction in sticking your hands in the dirt: an intimacy with the land on which we live. No matter how small or large your kitchen garden, it can feed your belly, heart, and mind.

Loganita Farms was started as a family venture to grow food for our neighbor, the renowned Willows Inn on Lummi Island. For the past several years, head gardener Mary von Krusenstiern has worked closely with chef Blaine Wetzel, whose gorgeous food tastes—to me—like this very place. At Loganita, we work to get high yields from little land, to conserve water, to nurture soil health, and to use earth-friendly products. Mary, Chelsee, Shelli, and Katie all tend the garden with love, which I believe makes the plants grow stronger and taste better.

Some of the children in our lives—Leo, Fran, Eliza, Trell, Seli'—are pictured in these pages. They fill this garden, and those we tend at our various homes—with play and laughter. Family and friends often drop by. (You'll see neighbor Al in one of Kristen's beautiful illustrations.)

This *Kitchen Garden Companion* is our way of sharing our experience and pleasure with you. Here, we aim to give you an overview of how you can start a garden, or get more from your existing garden, with as little time and as much enjoyment as possible. Although we're in the Salish Sea region, Mary's expert tips and techniques can be used wherever you are. The vegetables that we have selected are easy to source, and they grow well in many climates. We hope that you treat this book as a companion, that you take it with you from kitchen to garden and back again. Enjoy!

Julie Trimingham
CO-OWNER OF *Loganita Farms*

In the early spring of 2005 I arrived at a small farm located near Fairbanks, Alaska. I had no experience, and soaked up every bit of knowledge I could. My first day on the job we harvested overwintered parsnips. I was impressed that they could survive the harsh, Alaskan winters. That night we had a wonderful farm dinner of roasted overwintered vegetables seasoned with dried herbs. The next morning we began preparing the soil and getting the first spring plantings in the ground, including parsnips. This was one of my "ah ha!" moments, when I realized the beauty of the seasons and the magic of a little seed. We had come full circle: we were being nourished by last season's bounty while planting the seeds that would feed us later this year. I was hooked, and I haven't stopped growing food since.

PLANNING AS A
FORM OF DREAMING

A few years ago, we wanted to till a second half-acre field at Loganita. We spent the next year watching light patterns, taking soil tests, and, because we live in a part of the country that receives considerable rainfall, watching drainage patterns. With the information we gathered, we began drawing out a plan, sketching out irrigation lines and fencing, and dreaming our little half-acre field into reality.

You can't beat curiosity and observation when it comes to planning your space. Walk around your neighborhood and see what others have done in situations like yours. Visit your local library and check out gardening books and magazines. Seek out inspiration wherever you can and give yourself permission to dream about what is possible, something that is both creative enough to excite you and realistic enough to be successful.

As you begin to lay a foundation for your culinary garden, it's helpful to consider a few key elements:

- Where will you plant your garden?
- How big do you want it to be?
- Does it make most sense to grow food in containers, raised beds, or in the ground?

Site it strategically, taking sunlight, soil, and water into consideration.

Siting: Sun, Dirt, Water

All plants require sunlight to grow but differ in their needs for duration and intensity. Watch the way light falls across your landscape in different seasons and at different times of day. Don't be discouraged if your yard isn't constantly bathed in sunshine; many things thrive in dappled light. In the Northwest's temperate climate, we generally think of Southern exposure as ideal because it offers the most light, but in hotter areas this can prove to be too intense for some plants.

Plants that need *full sun* want a bright, sunny location with at least six hours of direct sunlight daily. *Partial sun* plants need three to six hours of sun each day. *Partial shade* plants require direct shade during the brightest times of day. *Shade* plants need indirect or filtered light to deep shade, with direct sunlight for less than three hours a day.

If your yard is like most, soil quality differs depending on where you dig. You might want to take out your spade for a few exploratory ventures to help you gain a sense of your soil type(s). Is your soil rocky, or sandy, or rich with nutrients? If you're planning to plant into containers or build raised beds, start researching your local soil supply options. Most local nurseries and hardware stores sell bags of potting soil for small-scale container planting, and a variety of soil mixes can be purchased by the truckload at landscape supply companies.

Consider where you'll connect hoses and fill watering cans—it's helpful to site your garden close to a water source. If designing an in-ground garden, take time to observe drainage patterns and look for locations that drain well and don't have standing water.

SOIL

The earth we walk on should be alive. Healthy soil is teeming with microbes that help plants access the food they need. We use compost and fertilize with organic soil amendments to keep our dirt healthy, rich, and fertile. (Many farmers and gardeners use the words "soil" and "dirt" interchangeably. We say things like "You've got great dirt here!" or "We're tilling up new dirt next season.") Each year, as crops deplete available nutrients from the ground, it is important to replenish those nutrients so next year's plants will have what they need to be in top form.

Most people don't recognize that plant roots actually grow in the spaces between the soil particles. If you've ever tried to grow something in hard dirt, you know it isn't easy. When soil is compacted, nutrients aren't readily available to your plants. As you enrich soil with compost and other amendments, you improve its structure, which helps to create balanced drainage and nutrient retention. The result? Healthier, happier plants.

Your plants need both macro- and micronutrients to produce a healthy and prolific crop. The primary macronutrients needed are nitrogen, phosphorous, and potassium (N-P-K). When shopping for organic amendments look for the N-P-K analysis written on the bag or box. Essential to healthy growth, but needed in smaller amounts, are secondary macronutrients: calcium, magnesium, and sulphur. Micronutrients are needed in trace amounts but are just as important for sustained crop health. Common micronutrients include zinc, iron, copper, manganese, boron, molybdenum, and choline.

At Loganita, we use native soil in our in-ground plots and manufactured soil in our raised beds. At the beginning of each season, we send soil samples to a soil analyst, who gives us a clear breakdown of the nutrient levels in our soil and the amendment recommendations for it. A simple soil test can save a lot of heartache. You can scratch your head all season wondering what's wrong, or you can find out exactly what macro- and micronutrients your ground needs to be able to be a successful veggie garden and then amend the soil accordingly. Things like boron deficiency or too much phosphorus have negative effects, and it's much easier to deal with soil issues before the plants are in the ground rather than after your crops are growing and you start to see problems.

It's worth it to spring for a professional soil test instead of opting for the cheaper do-it-yourself soil tests. The overall cost for professional analysis is nominal, and the results provide a level of specificity that helps ensure you're offering the best possible environment for your plants. Call your local agricultural extension or Master Gardener program to find a recommended source for soil testing in your area.

Manufactured Soil

If you're gardening in a raised bed or container, or your native soil is contaminated, chances are you'll be using manufactured soil. Manufactured soil is available by the truckload at many garden and landscape supply stores. Purchasing manufactured soil is a great way to get a head start and have an "instant garden," but we suggest proceeding with caution when choosing which soil to buy. Do your research and ask around for recommendations. Question the manufacturer about the materials used to make the soil (many manufactured soils tend to be heavy in sand and bark), and ask for a nutrient analysis. Because soil health is the foundation of plant health, it is worth it to buy the best you can get. And just because it's store-bought soil doesn't mean it has all the nutrients you'll need for a successful crop. We recommend a soil test so you know exactly what nutrients you'll need to add (or avoid adding).

Loganita dirt is a part of me.
Not only is it under my nails, it
is constantly on my mind as I
fret about how to best nurture
the crops in our four distinct growing
areas. My world consists of the Raised
Beds, the Greenhouses, the Lower Field, and the
Upper Field. Every growing area has vastly different
soil, each with its own particular needs. I carry
on a relationship with the ground in each of these
plots, continually improving, maintaining, and getting
to know their distinct personalities. And, just as
much as I shape the life of the soil, the soil in turn
shapes me. This dirt in our little acre feeds my soul,
fills my belly, and earns me a living. And while
Loganita dirt is a part of my life, it is also a
part of my son's life, as I worked the land during
my pregnancy and am now raising him among the
rows of vegetables and freshly tilled ground.

BEDS

Depending on your living situation and your gardening desires, you'll likely be planting into some variation of an in-ground plot, a raised bed, or a container.

In-Ground Plots

If you have beautiful, native soil and the ability to create an **in-ground plot**, by all means, do!

Whether you're working with an established garden plot or creating a garden bed where grass once was, come spring, you'll have some weeds to remove in preparation for planting. If you're pulling weeds from an established garden bed, count yourself lucky. Using a hori hori or spade, that tangled mess is relatively simple to remove—just remember to pull the weeds up by their roots and remove them from the garden.

Establishing a fresh bed where grass once was requires a bit more effort. You'll need to remove the sod layer by digging or smothering, then till the soil by hand or with a rototiller.

Digging produces immediate results, but we won't lie, it's a true workout! You should water the area prior to digging so the soil is moist, not waterlogged. Using an edger or spade, cut the sod into 1-foot-wide strips, then pry a fork or spade just beneath the roots and lift the strip up in 1- to 2-foot lengths. A sod cutter, available for rent from most hardware stores, can be a helpful alternative to hand-digging. Shake off any excess dirt and either transplant the sod or compost it. Remove any rocks from the soil and use a garden fork or broad-fork to work the soil until it is fluffy. Because you've just removed valuable organic material, as well as lowered the topsoil level, you should fill it back in with good-quality compost. Be sure to send in a soil sample, and follow the specific soil amendment recommendations.

If you're smothering sod, we suggest using silage tarp from your local farm store. (We've tried sheet mulching with cardboard and found it less effective.) Regardless of what you use, the goal is to eliminate light, making photosynthesis impossible, thus killing the grass without removing organic material. Silage tarp provides a continuous cover and has the added benefit of heating up the soil, which speeds up the decomposition process. Put silage tarp down in the summer and let it sit all year until the following spring. You'll then be able to rototill or hand-work the soil with a garden fork or broad-fork.

Tilling with a rototiller is a smart option for larger spaces, after the sod has been removed. Make passes with a smaller tiller for established gardens, but use a heavier rear tine tiller for new gardens. Many local hardware stores rent tillers by the day. While tilling has the potential to pulverize soil structure and can bring dormant weed seeds to the surface, it has the benefit of retaining organic material. Keep in mind, you're looking to enhance soil structure, not destroy it.

Raised Beds

Ideal for homes where an in-ground garden bed is not possible, a raised bed is a relatively simple project to tackle, even for inexperienced builders. Though it costs a bit of money up front in materials and soil, a raised bed offers a tidy, semi-permanent growing space that is easy to weed and mow around. When selecting the wood you'll use, think about longevity—a raised bed can be made quite cheaply with found wood, but better-quality lumber can last longer. While cedar is a great choice for longevity, fir is an affordable and durable option.

If you're building a raised bed on a concrete pad, you should put a layer of rocks under the soil for drainage. For most raised beds of any decent size, it makes sense to load up a truck or trailer with manufactured soil by the yard instead of purchasing individual bags of soil.

Containers

Start looking around different neighborhoods and you'll notice renegade gardens everywhere. All around you, people are making good use of old bathtubs, plastic buckets, wooden boxes, whiskey barrels, and other actual or invented garden containers. Container gardening is quick to gratify, easy to re-site, and a great place to start if you're just trying your hand at gardening.

Keep in mind that any container you intend to plant into will need drainage holes. Most purchased containers already have these, but if you're creating your own container, you may need to drill the holes yourself. Since you'll be harvesting food from your container garden, avoid choosing containers (and building materials) that could leach toxins into your planting soil.

as I walk out into the garden

It was two young farm girls who clued me in. The girls believed that, each night, garden fairies came out and made the plants grow with the touch of their wands. Every day as I walk out into the garden with my first cup of coffee, I take note of each crop's progress, what needs to get harvested, and what needs special attention. I look for possible harvest gaps and make a list of crops to succession plant, to ensure the longest possible harvest window. Before I get cracking on my to-do list, I sit in the garden and marvel at what the garden fairies have wrought overnight.

SHELTER

Row Cover

If you look at Loganita in the spring, you'll see a field covered in white. We cover most of our crops with floating row cover, a long, lightweight, breathable fabric "sheet" that drapes across your garden beds, allowing you to loosely tuck tiny seedlings under an extra layer of warmth and protection.

Row cover acts as a physical barrier against harsh weather, birds, and some of our most common garden pests. We cover all of our brassica crops to protect them from the imported cabbage moth, and we cover all crops that attract flea beetles. It is helpful to separate your crops in the bed according to row cover needs, keeping crops that benefit from row cover together. Put crops like edible flowers that don't need any row cover at the very ends of beds.

Row cover comes in different weights and sizes. The mid-weight all-purpose row cover that we use at Loganita raises the soil temperature by 4 degrees. A heavier-grade row cover designed for overwintering crops raises the temperature a bit higher.

Secure your row cover with rocks, scoops of dirt, or staples along the outside of your garden bed to prevent the wind from tangling it. Row cover can either rest gently on top of the foliage or, for plants that don't like moisture on their leaves, be secured above the plants with wire hoops.

Quick Hoops

Low tunnels, or "quick hoops," are inexpensive, instant greenhouses that go directly over your garden beds. Unlike row cover, low tunnels are constructed from

The ongoing love and protection that young things everywhere need

clear plastic, which is heavier and impermeable to moisture. Low tunnels let sunlight through and can increase temperatures to the point that it may be necessary to lift the sides of the plastic (or remove it altogether) during the hottest parts of the day.

If you do your research, you'll find many different ways to construct low tunnels. One such quick hoop is offered at the back of this book, in the "Nitty-Gritty" section.

Greenhouses

At Loganita, we are lucky enough to have four greenhouses, which we use for starting seeds and growing plants that are more sensitive or require hotter temperatures, and for simply extending our growing season. Basil, tomatoes, peppers, tomatillos, and eggplants all thrive under the protection a greenhouse affords. If you happen to have a greenhouse, or the space and resources to construct one, you'll be able to beautifully control your growing environments.

TOOLS

A friend of mine dug her first garden with a kitchen spoon. While this may have been the right choice for her at the time, tool selection really does make a huge difference in your overall gardening experience. Here are some of our favorite tools for making gardening easier.

Once your garden is workable, connecting directly with the soil with **your bare hands** is a great way to take stock of your soil quality and moisture levels, and an easy way to dig up weeds. Try ditching the garden gloves for a day and literally get in touch with your garden.

If I had to play favorites, the **hula hoe** would be my golden child. It's nothing more than a sharp steel stirrup blade attached to a long handle, but it skims just below the surface of the soil and makes weed removal effortless. It allows for forward and backward movement while keeping the soil intact.

A great choice for small weeds, the **trapezoid hoe** touts a sharp, beveled blade that allows you to cut young weeds precisely at their roots.

The **hori hori** is a stainless steel Japanese garden tool with a sharp point for digging. I use the hori hori for weeding and transplanting. Hands down, it's my most versatile hand tool.

Harvest knives come in a lot of shapes and sizes. We like the Victorinox brand of harvest knives for efficient cutting of greens. Plus they're extremely affordable and easy to replace.

If you plan on doing any amount of digging, a **spade** is a smart tool for the job. It's just like a shovel but has a pointed end instead of a flat end, making it a better tool for getting under the soil. I like the short-handled spades. They're lighter and easier to use.

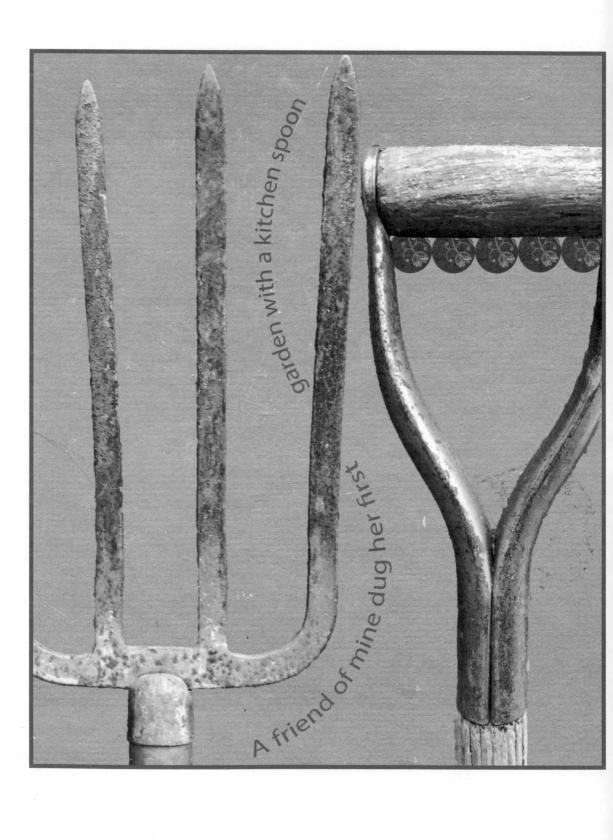

garden with a kitchen spoon

A friend of mine dug her first

A **straight garden rake** (not to be confused with a leaf rake) makes satisfyingly flat seed beds and garden beds and is a handy tool for removing debris from beds after weeding.

Felcos are the industry standard for consistently priced, well-designed, and long-lasting **pruners**. They are an upfront investment but, if taken care of properly, can last a lifetime.

The **broad-fork** and **garden forks** are great cultivation tools for manually breaking up dense soil, aerating the soil, and improving drainage. A broad-fork works well for larger plots, as it allows you to step on the crossbar to drive the tines into the ground. You can then draw the tines up through the soil while keeping the soil layers intact. Garden forks work well for cultivating manufactured soil and are smaller in size than broad-forks, making them ideal for small spaces. Both the broad-fork and garden forks are also helpful harvest tools for root crops and potatoes.

It was January, and I fired
up the rototiller.
I knew I shouldn't, but I
had an overwhelming
urge to get a head start
on the season, even though
the soil was half frozen. I already
knew about the ill effects of working the
soil too early and could easily count off
the reasons why, but that didn't stop me from
hoping that if I got an extra-early start
I would get an extra-early crop. After
rototilling, I used a garden rake to pull the
cold, wet soil over several rows of spinach seed.
After several weeks of lifting up the row cover
and digging through the soil for any signs of a
sprouted seed, I finally spotted the first leaves.
Several more weeks went by and the plants

just sat there, hardly growing at all. And then, one morning I eagerly lifted up the row cover and couldn't believe what I saw: the spinach was bolting! This meant I had to start over. A warmer, drier time of year was here, and so I raked out the bed, made rows, and once again planted the spinach. The days were longer, the birds were chirping, buds on the trees were emerging, and several days of sun had dried out the ground. The soil was ready, and this second time around I ended up with nice, big bunches of spinach.

WHEN TO PLANT

Remember that each season will be different and each climate is different. Even within the same regional area, timing can change depending on the particular elements at work in your garden. Our ground at Loganita is usually ready to plant in early April, but our farmer friend on the other side of the island has wetter soil that prevents her from planting a garden until Memorial Day. Notice the nuances of your garden and you'll find a rhythm that makes sense.

Soil temperature is important. Many seed packets say "seed as early as soil can be worked." This can be a bit deceiving. Just because you *can* work the soil doesn't mean that you *should*. Instead, wait until your dirt is ready. Organic growers rely on soil amendments for fertilizer, and those soil amendments rely on soil microbes to break them down and make nutrients available to the plants. If you plant before the soil has warmed up, while it is still wet and clumpy, those seeds won't get the nutrients they need to be healthy. If you plant a seed when the ground is adequately warm and dry, that seed is more likely to grow into a healthy plant that can naturally defend itself from pests and disease.

Understanding **days to maturity** can be a handy tool for garden planning. If we know the Willows wants a specific variety of cherry tomatoes in the second week in July, and we know that variety takes about 120 days to mature, we do the math and count backward to determine that we'll need to start seeds in the greenhouse in early March.

Open up your harvest window. Paying close attention to the "days to maturity" listed on your seed packets can also help you stagger the timing of your harvests and make the most of your growing season. Some veggies, like tomatoes, take around 70 days or longer to reach maturity, while others, like mixed greens, are ready to eat in less than 30 days. If your garden includes crops that are quick to mature as well as crops that take a bit longer, you'll ensure you have an assortment of veggies throughout your growing season.

Frost dates are the average date of the first and last frost of the season. You can look up your frost dates online by entering your zip code. Plan to plant seeds and transplants *after* the last frost and with consideration for the first frost at the end of the summer season. Knowing your first frost date at the end of summer allows you to count backward and determine planting windows. If you planted squash in August, there's no way it would make it to maturity before getting zapped by the first frost of the season.

Seed packets and the "Chart of All Things" at the back of this book can give you a general sense of when to plant a particular vegetable. With time and attention to seasonal patterns, you'll develop an intuitive sense of when to plant your culinary garden.

Make the most of what you've got

HOW TO PLANT

Ideally, by the time you're out in your garden with seed packets and starts, you'll have a sketch or a mental map of your kitchen garden. You'll know what you're going to plant based on what you'd like to eat, and you'll have thought about which plants you'll need to plant only once and which you'll be planting several times throughout the season in order to ensure a continuous harvest. The "Chart of All Things" at the back of this book will remind you what each plant needs and what each plant offers. Before you get your hands dirty, here are some considerations for how to plant your garden.

Make the most of what you've got. Even the smallest gardens hold the potential to yield bountiful veggies if you follow a few simple principles. At just over an acre, our farm at Loganita is considered quite small by most standards. By adopting some basic organizing principles, we're able to crank an incredible amount of produce out of our little farm.

- ❀ **Dense plantings:** You can pack a lot of veggies into a small amount of space if you plan things right. Generally, plants can be grown closer together than the seed packets indicate when given good soil and consistent watering. With time and observation, you'll learn how to take liberties with spacing.
- ❀ **Vertical planting:** If you're limited on space, create more of it by going up rather than out. Trellises require only minimal space in the garden, but open up a whole new level of productivity for plants like pole beans, peas, and cucumbers.

Harvest summer squash as needed all season. When they stop producing, pull plants and plant quick-growing radishes and salad turnips for fall harvest.

Acorn winter squash grow in an upright bush— a great choice for a small garden.

❀

Potatoes, carrots, beets, parsley: harvest as needed all season.

❀

After harvest, replant onion and celery spaces with spinach or lettuce.

❀

Carrots and beets: harvest as needed all season.

❀

Allow cucumbers to spill over the edge of the bed.

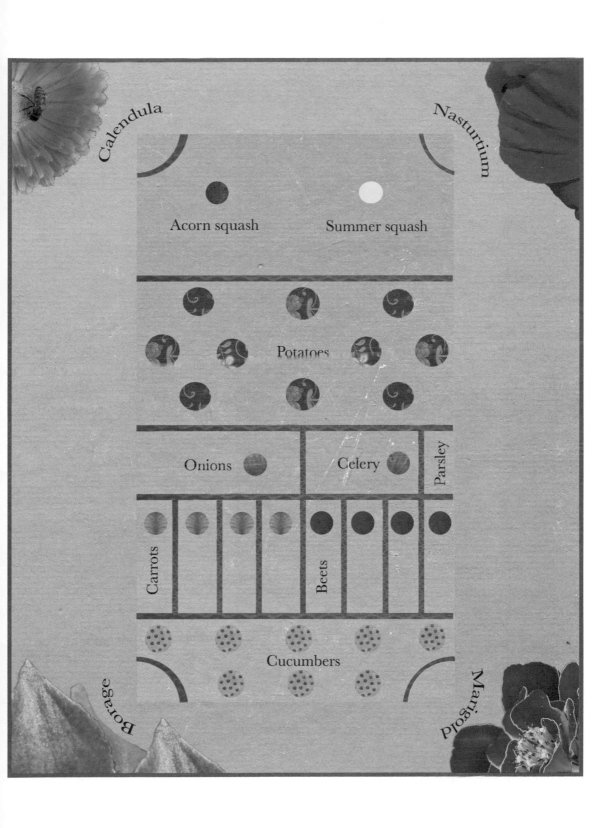

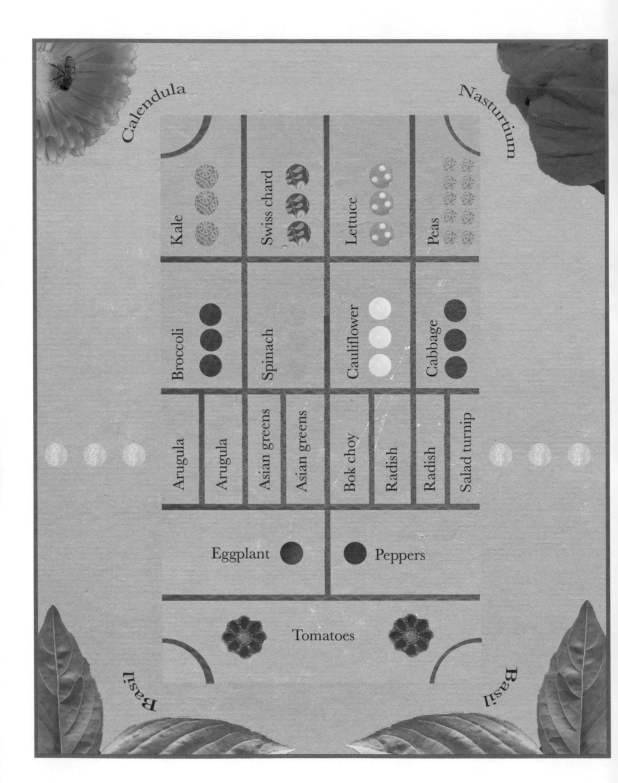

Kale and Swiss chard: leave in all season and harvest as needed.

When lettuce is done, replant with another round
of radishes and salad turnips.

Pull peas when they are done producing. Replant with
turnips and rutabagas for fall harvest.

❁

Harvest off broccoli plants all season.

When spinach, cauliflower, and cabbage are done,
replant with quick-growing greens.

❁

When these quick-growing crops (arugula, Asian greens, bok choy,
radish, salad turnips) are done, replant with green beans.

❁

Pull eggplants, peppers, tomatoes, and basil when they stop producing.
Replant with quick-growing greens for fall harvest.

There are two ways to get your plants going:

- ✿ **Direct seeding** is when you plant a seed straight into your prepared garden bed.
- ✿ **Transplants** (or **starts**) are young plants that you buy, acquire from a friend, or grow yourself). Transplants have been started from seed in pots and are now ready to plant out in your field, containers, a raised bed, or a greenhouse.

To prepare your garden bed for direct seeding or transplanting, rake out the soil until it's smooth, weed-free, and easy to "draw" rows in. Seed rows are simply straight, evenly spaced guides for where seeds and transplants will go. You can draw lines with a rake, your finger, or a piece of wood. Straight lines make weeding fast and efficient, as you can simply pull a hula hoe or rough up the soil with your hands right between the rows. For a large garden, row markers or even a hand seeder makes the job of direct seeding more efficient.

Direct Seeding

If you're **direct seeding**, make sure the soil is free of weeds, light, and fluffy. Give the soil a gentle watering a few hours prior to planting, letting the water thoroughly percolate through the bed. Check the soil before planting—its moisture level should feel like a well-wrung-out sponge.

Seeds generally like to be planted twice as deep as the seed itself is wide. Big seeds like winter squash are a cinch—just poke them about an inch beneath the soil surface, then cover them over with soil. Some seeds are especially tiny; we sprinkle the seeds into rows and then use a garden rake to cover them with a light dusting of soil. For crops that do best with a little bit of space between each seedling, we make sure to thin the crop after the seeds have germinated. Some crops (like salad mix) don't mind being crowded, so we leave them alone. Refer to our spacing recommendations in the "Chart of All Things" at the back of this book. To aid in germination and protect from pests, cover your freshly seeded crops with row cover.

Transplants

Come spring, you'll see veggie starts for sale at the local grocery stores and garden centers. While many crops are easy to get going on a card table in the backyard or a windowsill, it can be helpful to purchase crops that benefit from an extra-early start—tomatoes, peppers, and eggplants—from a garden center or your local farmers' market.

A seed's entire purpose is to grow.

The ideal transplant is a healthy-looking plant with a well-established root system. Leaves should be bright and perky, not yellowed or discolored from disease or nutrient deficiency. Stay away from veggie starts that have begun to flower or that are root-bound (meaning the roots have outgrown their container and are a solid, tangled mass).

Once you get your transplants home, get them in the ground as soon as possible. If the transplants are dry, give them a good watering and let the water soak all the way down to the base of the roots. Squeeze the bottom of the container to loosen the roots and pull gently at the base of the stem to dislodge the plant start.

Dig a hole that is big enough to accommodate the transplant and plop the transplant into the soft dirt so the base of the stem is level with the rest of the soil. Firmly pat down soil around the base of the stem. At Loganita we do a transplant soak before setting plants in the ground. Prior to planting, we mix up a batch of organic fish fertilizer and soak each transplant before planting out. This gives them a boost of nutrients that helps them transition from the pot to their permanent home in the soil.

In the initial days after transplanting, plant starts have a whole new world to get used to. Their roots are exploring beyond the confines of their growing containers and the leaves become fully exposed to the elements. Watch your plants closely during this tender passage, and water for a short amount of time each day to help the root systems adjust to their new environment. To ease the transition from pot to soil, we cover our transplants with row cover to provide a protected environment away from the harsh weather and pests.

Seeds and How to Start Them

Starting your own seeds is one of the most gratifying and exciting parts of gardening. Not only does it allow you to be a part of the entire process of your garden's life cycle, it also opens up a whole world of varieties that you're unlikely to find at your local garden store. Anyone can start seeds, no greenhouse required. You simply need to know a few basics of seed starting.

Open pollinated varieties are pollinated by wind, insects, birds, humans, or other natural means. The seeds from open pollinated varieties can be saved from year to year because they will grow "true" to the parent plant, as long as care is taken to prevent cross-pollination with other varieties of the same species. **Heirloom varieties** are open pollinated varieties that have been handed down for generations.

Hybrid varieties are the intentional crosses between two different parent varieties. They are species made possible by controlled pollination through human intervention. Commercially available hybrid seeds are often labeled as FI hybrids. These seeds must be purchased every year because the seed saved from an FI hybrid will not produce true to the parent.

You can plant seeds in anything from egg cartons to yogurt containers. All you need is a container that holds soil and has drainage (and if it doesn't have drainage, just poke holes and make your own). If you're in the habit of buying starts, save your discarded plastic cell packs and reuse them. Or you can buy new cell packs at most garden centers. When you're filling a container with potting soil, give it a firm tap on a hard surface before you start seeding so that the soil settles. Plop the seed in, and then cover with a light dusting of potting soil or vermiculite. You want the seed to be fully covered, but not smothered.

Seeds need **light** to sprout! A south-facing window is an ideal location to start seeds. If you have such a setup, just be sure to rotate seeds periodically so all sides receive light. There are tons of fancy LED and fluorescent light systems out there that do a great job of mimicking natural light where there is none, but if natural light is an option there's no sense in not using it.

Make sure to **site your seeds in a place where you can check on them daily**. Tiny seedlings require water a few times a day, so put them in a place that is easy to access and where you'll notice them.

Proper watering of seedlings in a greenhouse (or on your windowsill) is important. We have a misting system in our seed-starting greenhouse. In the beginning, **seeds will want to be watered** multiple times a day. Soil should be allowed to dry out slightly between waterings but never dry out completely. As seeds begin to germinate and their first leaves appear above the soil surface, their root systems are also maturing and they'll need less-frequent watering. Under-watering prevents the roots at the bottom from getting the hydration they need. Overwatering leads to disease and rot. Maintain even, consistent watering, making sure to hydrate all corners of the growing medium, to help get seeds off to their best start. Watch your plants closely, and adjust your daily watering to their specific needs.

Label each of your seeds with a seed tag that notes the date you planted it and the variety name. When it's time to transplant, this tag can accompany the plant to its new garden home.

A good potting mix should not be too heavy or too light—the former will suffocate the seeds, while the latter is likely full of fillers with little nutrient value. Opt for a balanced mix that is properly weighted and has a healthy combination of organic ingredients such as compost, bonemeal, fish meal, and blood meal. Look for ingredients like perlite, vermiculite, or sand that help increase drainage and reduce compaction. Peat is a common ingredient added to increase water absorption. We avoid potting soil mixes with synthetic ingredients and stick with those that are approved for use in organic agriculture.

If you notice your plants looking a bit hungry after sitting in their pots for a long time, you might try fertigating with an organic all-purpose feed. To fertigate means to thoroughly water your plants with a water-soluble or liquid fertilizer.

Once the roots of your seedlings begin to outgrow their pots, you can **transplant** them into larger containers ("potting up" or "up potting"). A good way to check the development of the root structure on a mature seedling is to gently pull the seedling by the base of its stem. If you've planted into plastic cells, you can pull the entire plant up and examine the root structure. If the root structure maintains its shape, is dense, and is well developed, it is probably ready to plant.

When your seedlings are ready to leave the nursery, gently introduce them to the cruel world (direct sunlight, wind, and other natural elements). This period of transition is called **hardening off**. Over the course of a few days, bring the seedlings outside for increasing lengths of time. Start with a few hours and gradually increase the duration of exposure. After a few days, they'll be ready to plant outside.

After transplanting, seedlings should be immediately **watered in**.

Thinking ahead to your next season, store your unused seeds correctly. Seeds love a cool, dark place like a closet, basement, or garage. We keep ours in a sealed Tupperware container in a windowless, unheated room. When properly stored, seeds can last a long time.

Who belongs in the garden?

TEND AND DEFEND

Once you've planted your seeds and transplants, you'll need to give them the ongoing love and protection that young things everywhere need. Plants are fed by soil, sun, and water. Assessing soil health and siting your garden are things you will have done prior to planting. You should amend your soil on an as-needed basis, and water regularly, maybe even daily, depending on where you are.

You'll also need to protect your growing garden from weeds and pests. Prevention is the best cure: strong, healthy, well-fed plants are less likely to be taken down by disease or pest damage. That said, we like to inspect for pest or disease once a week and nip any problems in the bud.

Feeding

You might find that the foliage on some of your plants is discolored or malformed due to a nutrient imbalance. Nutrient imbalance will also cause some crops to bolt prematurely. Bolting is when plants focus all their energy into going to seed in a final attempt to reproduce. Your crops will eventually go to seed as a part of their natural cycle; early bolting is an indicator that you should put extra care into your soil, in an effort to avoid issues when you plant the next crop.

Go organic: Ask for products listed with an OMRI (Organic Materials Review Institute) stamp at your local garden store. Anything with this stamp is certified for use on organic farms. We have found that organic is best for the Earth, for the plants, and for our own bodies.

Watering

When people tell us there's a problem in their garden, it often comes down to one of two things: soil or water. A good soil test offers straightforward solutions to nutrient deficiencies in the soil, but addressing water absorption in your plants can be a little trickier. It requires cultivating balanced soil structure and adopting consistent, mindful irrigation methods.

You need look no further for signs of watering deficiency or excessiveness than the plants themselves. Plants that don't get enough water tend to be wilted and fall over because their cells are not hydrated and lack the turgor pressure to hold themselves upright. Overwatering plants is a more common problem. Roots growing in waterlogged soil have a difficult time absorbing the oxygen they need to survive; they essentially drown. Stunted growth, yellowed leaves, spots, rot, and disease can all be signs of overwatering.

You need to get your hands dirty to really **assess soil moisture levels**. Grab a hand trowel and dig into the soil, deep enough that you're collecting soil from the same root zone as the plants in your garden. Collect a ball of soil in your hands—ideally, it will feel about as wet as a well-wrung-out sponge and will fall apart if you bounce it in your palm a few times. Once you're familiar with your soil, you can replace the trowel test with a finger test and stick a few fingers into the soil to assess how wet or dry it is.

Watering by hand or with sprinklers is a breeze in terms of infrastructure, but it requires your precious time. Timed drip irrigation requires the most infrastructure, but we stand behind it wholeheartedly and encourage you to try it. Drip irrigation gets water directly to the root zone and conserves water. While it takes a little time up front, it saves a great deal of time in the long run. At the back of this book, in the "Nitty-Gritty" section, you'll find more information on the pros and cons of different watering methods, as well as instructions on how to set up a timed drip system.

Regardless of what method you choose:

- ❀ **Constancy is key.** Once you've learned how your soil holds water (every garden is different), get on a schedule. At Loganita we water for

Constancy is key

a certain amount of time daily, and each of our plots requires a different amount of time. Our lower field drains easily, and we set the irrigation for a bit more time than for our upper field, which has a different soil structure that holds more water.

- ❀ **Water deeply**, so the water penetrates the root zone and encourages further root growth.
- ❀ **Adjust watering frequency based on daily temperatures and rainfall.** An extra-hot day likely means your plants will be thirsty for more water.
- ❀ Water in the early morning and late afternoon or evening to **reduce evaporation** and conserve water.
- ❀ **Water only as needed.** Pay attention to your plants and allow the soil to dry out slightly between waterings. Wilting plants often perk up when the heat of day has passed. If you're not sure, do a finger test and check the moisture level of your soil. Not sure if you've watered enough? Check your soil about two hours after watering, after the water has had time to percolate through.

Thinning

When direct seeding, you will often sow several seeds close together. You will need to thin the crop if you desire fully matured veggies. Thinning means that once the seeds have germinated and the seedlings are established, you'll pull some of the seedlings out so that others have room to grow. Often, the thinnings can be used in a stir-fry, a salad, a frittata, or some other yummy dish, so don't automatically assume they're compost!

Weeding

The "undesirables" of the plant world, weeds are simply plants that grow more vigorously than your intended crop and directly compete for nutrients and water. What constitutes a weed is up for interpretation. Dandelion greens, purslane, and wild sorrel are considered weeds by some, delicacies by others; wild foraged "weeds" are a favorite ingredient at the Willows, and, as you come to know the prevailing weeds in your garden, you may find a few unique ingredients to add to your salads.

We've never met a farmer who has managed to eliminate weeds from his or her culinary garden. Weeds needn't be a nemesis of your garden, but keeping them manageable requires regular attention.

One of the easiest ways to control weeds is to stop them before they get out of control. Weeding a small garden plot takes just a few minutes when weeds are in their infancy. Those same weeds can take several hours to remove if left uncontrolled. As part of your weekly tending, disturb the soil about ½ inch below the surface with a hula hoe or trapezoid hoe to intercept weeds before they have a chance to emerge. Once uprooted, young or non-emerged weeds can be left in the garden bed. Larger, established weeds are best removed and taken to the compost.

Baby seedlings are no match for unchecked weeds, and it is especially important to weed prior to direct sowing or transplanting, and once a week immediately after planting.

One of the most common questions I am asked is "How do you figure out what to plant and how much to plant?" Although I am taking notes throughout the season, my official planning process begins in November. Blaine and I sit down over coffee and begin to reflect on the previous growing season. We talk about what we had plenty of, what we need more of, what we'd like to do differently, what we'd like to keep the same. And then we start outlining the crop map and planning the menu for the following season. Yes, we are planning how many Caraflex cabbages will be delivered per day to coincide with the tuna harvest the following July, eight months away. We go down the list for every single crop, and, come December, we have a solid plan. Of course, there are variables and surprises, crop failures and bumper crops, but, in general, our late-fall planning session steers the ship. Thrown into the mix are experimental and trial crops. By January, I am placing seed orders, obtaining growing supplies, and starting up the new season.

WHAT TO PLANT

Choosing what to plant is as easy as thinking about what you like to eat or would like to eat more of, what you'll use often, and how much you are able to grow in the space you've allocated. There are endless types and styles of culinary gardens, from potted herb gardens full of rich tufts of basil and aromatic rosemary to "cut and come again" salad gardens that offer a continuous outpouring of greens all season long.

Here are a few guiding principles we've found helpful when you are selecting the varieties you'd like to plant.

Gardening zones: Each part of the country is assigned a gardening hardiness "zone" that indicates which plants thrive in a given region based on minimum winter temperatures. Loganita's location on Lummi Island is zone 8a, which means that we're able to plant seeds and starts that are hardy to our zone and farther south. Most seed packets indicate hardiness zones, and seed starts purchased in your area are generally suited to your zone. Hardiness zones for different regions are available online or from your local agricultural extension.

Spacing considerations: Tiny seeds can grow into giants. Watermelon and winter squash can easily overtake a garden. You might want to choose plants that offer more diversity and versatility in a smaller amount of space. Carrots, mixed greens, beets, and kale are examples of vegetables that don't hog the bed. You can also create vertical space in the garden by trellising plants like pole beans, peas, and cucumbers. When thinking about arranging plants in the garden, ensure that all plants have adequate access to light and aren't shading out their neighbors.

Thinking about your crops in the following categories can be helpful:

- **Instant gratification**: These veggies have a quick turnaround time and, from initial sowing to final harvest, often take less than 30 days.
- **Continuous** harvest: These veggies can stay in the ground and have a wide harvest window, offering a continuous harvest throughout the season.
- **Succession planting**: Time the plantings of these veggies a few weeks apart, leaving space in the garden for the next wave of planting. When one wave of veggies is finished, replant new veggies into the open space. Depending on the "days to maturity," some plants allow for multiple successions, while others will only allow for one or two.
- **"Cut and come again"** crops are those which you can harvest and then allow to grow back. Cut the entire plant 2 inches from the soil line when harvesting. I call this "giving the crop a haircut."
- **Single planting**: These veggies take a long time to reach maturity, but you'll often get a long harvest window.

The categories can overlap. For example, kale, Swiss chard, and broccoli are examples of "continuous harvest" crops but also are "succession planting crops," because you should put two plantings in: one in spring for summer harvest and one in summer for fall/winter harvest.

AN INDEX OF LOVE: OUR FAVORITE VEGGIES

These are some of our favorite veggies at Loganita. Most of these are easygoing plants that offer up deliciousness in a number of ways. An overview of each plant is presented here; the "Chart of All Things" at the back of this book indicates more technical specifics.

Here you'll see what we like to do with regard to direct seeding, starting seeds, and transplants. But, of course, any plant can be direct seeded, started in a cell pack, or bought as a transplant! We simply offer the methods we prefer for each plant at Loganita.

In the "Chart of All Things," we also indicate how we think of the plants, whether a plant is a good candidate for succession planting, can be "cut and come again," or if we tend to plant and harvest it only once. It's helpful to plan out which parts of your garden will see a few crops during a season and which parts will be dedicated to only one crop.

ARUGULA

Native to Southern Europe and Western Asia, this "cut and come again" salad green has a reputation in some countries as an aphrodisiac. Sometimes called "rocket" or "roquette," arugula seeds can be purchased as either a salad or a wild variety. Easy to harvest and grow, arugula is a spicy addition to salads and sandwiches.

Plant: Direct seed. Use row cover to aid in germination and protect from pests. Arugula is a cool-season crop and tends to bolt more easily in the summer months.

Common Pest(s): Slugs, flea beetles, birds.

Harvest: Expect two good harvests from a single planting.

Enjoy: Use the tender first-harvest leaves of arugula in salads. Its peppery flavor is especially good in salads tossed with a sweet fruit like apples or pomegranate and a hard or bleu cheese. Try sautéing arugula on its own in olive oil with a little salt and pepper. Add to sandwiches and as a finishing garnish on pizzas. Bolted arugula has a stronger flavor, and its greens make an excellent pesto.

Store and Preserve: Make an arugula pesto and freeze in ice cube trays to make individual pesto cubes. Store in an airtight container in the freezer.

ASIAN GREENS

Another "cut and come again" vegetable, Asian greens salad mixes are similar in growth habit to a traditional salad mix. Asian greens can be enjoyed raw or cooked, and make an easy substitution for napa cabbage or bok choy. There are many choices when it comes to which Asian greens to grow, and we encourage you to try several until you find your favorites. At Loganita, we have a list of varieties that the chefs ask us to grow year after year, each with its own distinct flavor and texture.

Plant: Direct seed. Use row cover to aid in germination and protect from pests. Plant once a month for continuous harvest.

Common Pest(s): Flea beetles, slugs, birds.

Harvest: With Asian greens, expect three to four good cuttings.

Enjoy: Greens can get out of control and grow fast, and a stir-fry is a sure way to use them up (and get your daily dose of vitamins). Asian greens salad mix can hold its own as a green salad or tossed in an Asian noodle salad with other veggies, sesame oil, soy sauce, and toasted seeds or nuts. Asian greens are also great to throw into a stir-fry just before finishing.

Store and Preserve: After cutting salad greens, wash and dry, then place in a plastic bag with a layer of paper towels to soak up any remaining moisture. Refrigerate.

BASIL

The chefs at the Willows first introduced me to the mini bush basil varieties. At first, I thought they would be tedious, and more of a garnish than a main ingredient. Instead, I found them to be packed with flavor and easy to use because they come off in dainty, delicate plumes that can easily be tossed into a salad or on a pizza. No chopping required! Because of their compact growing style, they are great for small spaces and container gardens.

Plant: Transplant. If greenhouse space is available, save a spot for basil, as it is a good crop to grow under cover. Basil likes to keep its leaves dry and enjoys warmth. Row cover is a great alternative if you don't have a greenhouse, but because basil is finicky about its leaves being wet, use wire hoops to keep the row cover from touching the leaves.

Harvest: For mini bush-type basils, harvest as you would for "cut and come again" greens: hold the top of the plant and cut across with a serrated knife, leaving a healthy amount of stem for new growth. For standard basil varieties, harvest individual leaves or cut whole stalks. While it's fine to harvest individual leaves and stalks as you need them, it is important to complete a full harvest before the crop begins to flower, in order to promote new growth.

Enjoy: Add to soups, salads, and sauces. Cut in a thin chiffonade and add to salads or scrambled eggs. Add whole leaves to finish stir-fries or pizza. Basil is the main ingredient of classic pesto, a great addition to sandwiches and pastas or drizzled as a garnish on a bowl of soup. Basil leaves tend to brown when cooked, so add basil to hot ingredients at the last moment so that it retains its vibrant color.

Store and Preserve: Basil pesto tastes amazing and freezes well. Freeze individual portions in ice cube trays, then transfer to an airtight freezer container. It can also be canned.

BEETS

This root vegetable contains an amazing organic compound called geosmin. Geosmin is responsible for the earthy smell in the air after a heavy rainfall in the spring. Humans are sensitive to small amounts of geosmin and can detect its scent even in trace amounts, which helps to explain why people have such polarized opinions about beets. Some love their sweet, earthy flavor, while others detest it. We're in the former category! Beets come in a variety of gorgeous colors, from golden to red to striped, and all parts of the beet can be used, including the top.

Plant: Direct seed or transplant. Use row cover to aid in germination and protect from pests.

Common Pest(s): Leaf miners, slugs, birds.

Harvest: You can begin harvesting beets as soon as the roots begin to swell, or wait until the roots reach their full growth about two months after seeding. Beets can also be grown for their greens; in that case, seed a bit more densely and harvest as soon as desired.

Enjoy: Roasted beets are our favorite on the farm, especially with a drizzle of balsamic vinegar. Grate raw beets into salads or make the traditional Ukrainian soup borscht. Beet greens are the most nutrient-dense part of the plant and can be added to stir-fries or used as a substitute for kale. Tiny beet thinnings can even be used in salads or as a garnish.

Store and Preserve: Beets will store well in a bucket of sand in the root cellar, or on your porch or in your garage. Just be sure to keep them out of freezing temperatures. Savory or sweet pickled beets are delicious.

BOK CHOY

Translated from Cantonese, *bok choy* means "white vegetable," a nod to its bright white stem. Originating in China, bok choy is a nutrient-dense cruciferous vegetable and is a delicious addition to sautés and Asian stir-fries.

Plant: Direct seed or transplant. Use row cover to aid in germination and protect from pests.

Common Pest(s): Flea beetles, slugs, birds.

Harvest: For large, juicy stemmed bok choy plants, start thinning as soon as the crop is well established. Toss the thinnings into a stir-fry, or cut them up for the salad bowl.

Enjoy: Braised bok choy is a bright addition to a noodle bowl. It can hold its own as a side dish, sautéed with a little garlic and drizzled with sesame oil. If cooked lightly, it has a distinctive crunch, similar to celery. Cook longer and it turns creamy.

Store and Preserve: Wash bok choy thoroughly before putting in the crisper drawer of your refrigerator. Dirt likes to hang out in the crevices around the stalk. Bok choy can also be blanched in boiling water for two minutes, plunged into a cold water bath, and frozen.

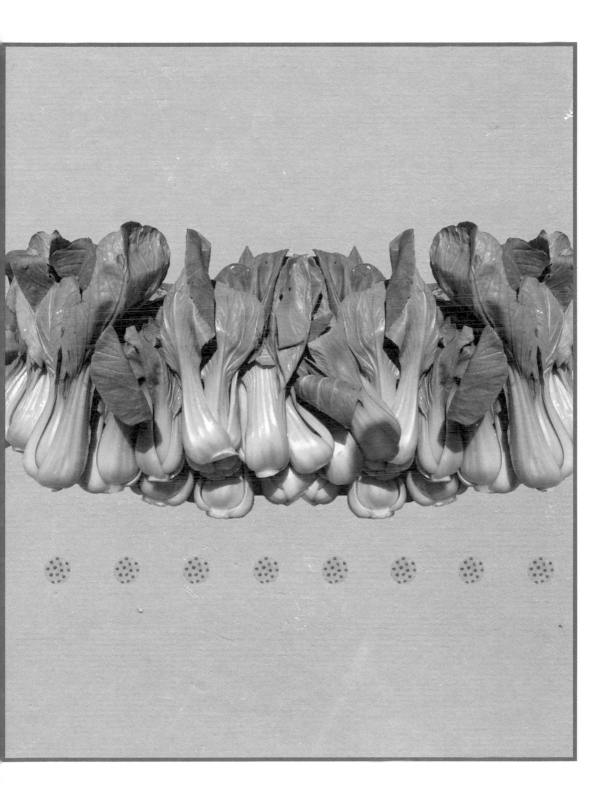

BROCCOLI

Our favorite variety of broccoli is De Cicco, an Italian heirloom broccoli that can be harvested all season from a single sowing. It is unique in its growing habit; instead of producing a main head, side shoots develop, which produce more medium-sized heads for harvest.

Plant: Transplant. Use row cover to aid in germination and protect from pests. If cabbage moths are persistent, keep the crop covered until harvest time.

Common Pest(s): Imported cabbage moth, aphids, slugs, birds.

Harvest: Most broccoli varieties produce one main head followed by several side shoots. Harvest side shoots regularly to encourage new growth.

Enjoy: Steam or roast broccoli with a bit of olive oil and salt, or toss in a stir-fry. Take care to keep broccoli's vibrant green color when cooking, and cook only until al dente. Broccoli can be enjoyed in its raw form, and it makes a mean raw salad—try chopping it finely and mixing with nuts, cranberries, and a light vinaigrette.

Store and Preserve: Another reason we love broccoli is that it can be frozen without blanching.

CABBAGE

Along with a number of other cruciferous vegetables, cabbage is sometimes called a "cole crop" because it developed from varieties of wild cabbage called "colewort" or field cabbage. A favorite for fermenting, we love to make a big crock of sauerkraut in the autumn for New Year's Day to start us off on the right foot in the new year. The pointy-headed cabbage Caraflex and Cur De Bue are Chef Blaine's favorite varieties.

Plant: Transplant. Use row cover to aid in germination and protect from pests. If cabbage moths are persistent, keep the crop covered until harvest time.

Common Pest(s): Imported cabbage moth, aphids, slugs, birds.

Harvest: You'll know that a cabbage head is ready to harvest when the leaves are wrapped tightly to form a head. Make sure to harvest when the heads are mature—if left to keep growing, they are susceptible to splitting when overgrown.

Enjoy: Excellent in a summer cole slaw, cabbage also makes a velvety soup if cooked with a little chicken stock and onion and pureed. Fermenting cabbage into sauerkraut is a delicious way to enjoy your summer crop in the middle of winter.

Store or Preserve: Fermenting is an ideal way to preserve cabbage. You can also blanch thinly sliced cabbage in boiling water for three minutes and freeze.

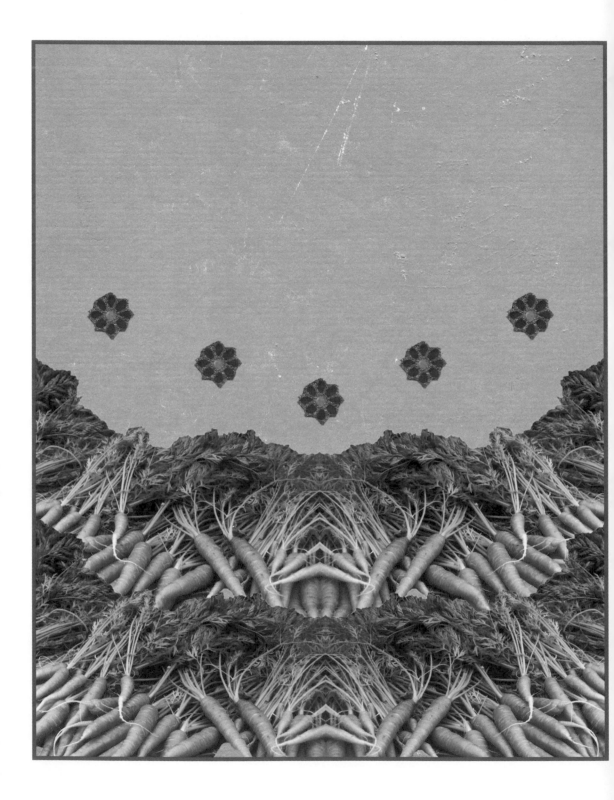

CARROTS

Carrots are one of our favorite crops to eat directly out of the garden. With colors ranging from traditional orange to purple and red, and an extended harvest window to boot, carrots are a fun and easy option for the culinary gardener. Stagger your carrot plantings if you want to be able to pluck carrots from the garden all summer long.

Plant: Direct seed. Use row cover to aid in germination and protect from pests.

Common Pest(s): Wireworms, slugs.

Harvest: Begin harvesting baby carrots as soon as the roots begin to swell. If you prefer a larger carrot, they reach their full potential size about two months after direct seeding.

Enjoy: Pureed carrot soup with a drizzle of reduced balsamic vinegar is one of my go-to recipes in the spring, when carrots are young, tender, and at their most flavorful. Grate carrots into your salad or roast in the oven with onions, beets, and other root vegetables for a savory winter side dish.

Store and Preserve: Carrots will hold in the ground during a typical Pacific Northwest winter, and they will also hold for quite some time in the root cellar or refrigerator. After harvesting carrots, be sure to cut off the carrot top greens immediately. During the first three months of storage, carrots actually increase their vitamin A content. Store carrots in sand in a cool location, safe from freezing, to keep them over the winter. You can also blanch and freeze carrots, quick-pickle with vinegar, or use a steam canner for long-term storage. A hot-water bath is not recommended for canning carrots.

CAULIFLOWER

A relative of kale and a member of the brassica family, the edible white flesh of the cauliflower is sometimes called the "curd" for its close resemblance to cheese curds. Cauliflower can be grown in four colors: white, green, orange, and purple. Varieties like Romanesco cauliflower grow into unique, prehistoric-looking heads and are rarely found in grocery stores—a great pick for the culinary home garden.

Plant: Transplant. Use row cover to aid in germination and protect from pests. If cabbage moths are persistent, keep the crop covered until harvest time.

Common Pest(s): Imported cabbage moth, aphids, slugs, wireworms, birds.

Harvest: You'll know that a cauliflower head is mature when it is firm and compact, and the buds are still tight and unopened. Make sure to harvest when the heads are mature—if left to keep growing, the buds will begin the process of flowering.

Enjoy: Steam or roast cauliflower florets with a drizzle of olive oil and some salt. Sauté with onions and curry powder for an Indian side dish, or gently simmer with chicken stock and puree into a soup. Cauliflower heads can also be pickled or eaten raw.

Store and Preserve: Blanch in boiling water for three minutes, then freeze. Cauliflower can be quick-pickled in a vinegar brine or canned in a hot-water bath for longer-term storage.

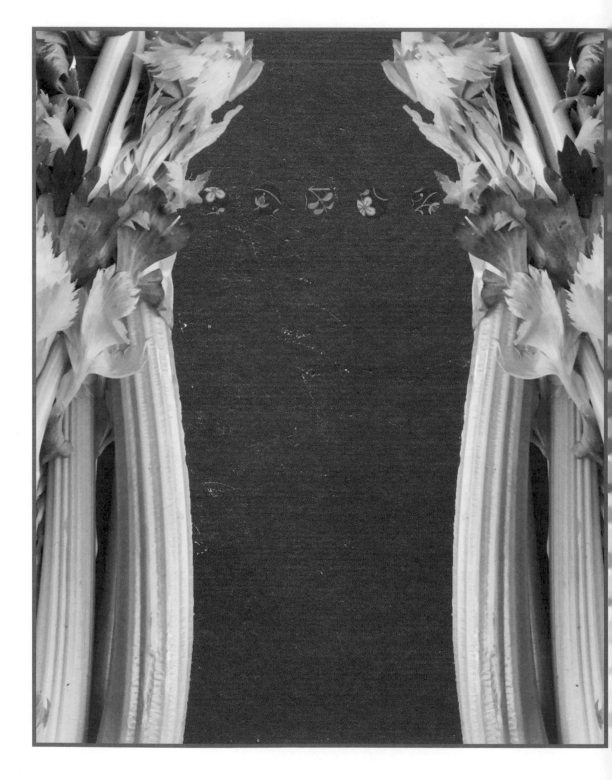

CELERY

One of the joys of a culinary garden is its ability to help us look at vegetables through a fresh lens. While most grocery celery is lackluster at best, home-grown celery is surprisingly delicious. Slightly sweet and crisp, we harvest fresh celery from the garden for flavorful soup stocks and use it as a mainstay in our juicing garden. On its own, it's a satisfying snack.

Plant: Transplant. Young celery plants tend to bolt if exposed to colder temperatures (below 60 degrees). To minimize bolting, we generally transplant in early May. Established celery plants can withstand one or two light frosts.

Common Pest(s): Aphids.

Harvest: Cut the whole plant, or harvest individual stalks. For a continuous harvest, plant three times, spacing the plantings one month apart.

Enjoy: Unadulterated garden-fresh celery is a cooling summer snack and makes an easy appetizer: any spread you can put on crackers also tastes great on celery. Shave into a salad with fennel, grains, nuts, and a light vinaigrette. Celery leaves also make a delicious simple syrup for mixed drinks or sorbets.

Store and Preserve: The best way to store celery in your fridge is whole and wrapped in aluminum foil, which, unlike plastic, doesn't trap in the ethylene that celery naturally gives off. For longer storage, blanch celery stalks in boiling water for three minutes, plunge into an ice-water bath, dry, and freeze. Frozen celery is ideal for soups and stews, but won't retain its crispness.

CILANTRO

All parts of the cilantro plant are edible, from seed to leaf to flower to root. The coriander seed is an essential ingredient in Indian cuisine, and its citrusy leaves are featured prominently in many Mexican dishes. We dry cilantro in bunches after it's gone to seed—a beautiful green bundle from which we harvest coriander seeds early in the winter. Cilantro is also a favorite of bees, and they flock to its flowers.

Plant: Direct seed or start in cell packs. If direct seeding, use row cover to aid in germination. Cilantro is notorious for bolting quickly and is sensitive to frost.

Common Pest(s): Slugs.

Harvest: Cut the entire crop 2 inches from the soil level and allow to grow back, or harvest individual leaves as needed.

Enjoy: Cilantro is an extraordinarily versatile herb. Its leaves and stems can be chopped and added to sauces, salads, and soups. Chopped leaves make a great pesto or a bright addition to guacamole. We love to add whole cilantro leaves to both Mexican and Asian-inspired soups. The coriander seed, which tastes nothing like the leaf, can be harvested and used when still young and green or when dried and brown.

Store and Preserve: Store in the fridge, wrapped in a slightly damp paper towel. The stems and leaves of the cilantro plant can be thrown right into a freezer bag without blanching. It holds its flavor surprisingly well. Store dried coriander seeds in a glass jar, or hang a bunch of drying coriander from the wall in the autumn, and harvest through the winter as needed.

CUCUMBERS

There are three types of cucumbers available for planting: slicing, seedless, and pickling. Within these types, there are plenty of varieties, most of them requiring pollination from another plant, as most cucumber plants are "self-incompatible." We've grown some unusual varieties of cucumbers at Loganita—gorgeous cucumbers that closely resemble a pear, and tiny cucumbers, no bigger than a kumquat, that pack an amazing crunch. These vining plants take up space and grow well on a trellis, where it is easier to keep an eye on the fruit as it grows and ripens.

Plant: Direct seed or transplant. To save space, try growing cucumbers vertically. Attach heavy-duty twine to overhead supports and pull the twine to the base of the plant. Attach the twine to the plant with plant clips. Every week, we "string up" the growing plants by using a clip to attach new growth to the twine. Cucumbers can also be trellised up wire fencing or wooden stakes. We like to use row cover to shelter the tender seedlings from erratic Pacific Northwest spring weather.

Common Pest(s): Root maggots, slugs, birds.

Harvest: Harvest often to encourage growth.

Enjoy: Simple sliced cucumbers with a sprinkling of salt is one of our favorite snacks at the farm. Cucumber is a great addition to salads but can also hold its own as a vinegar cucumber salad with a bit of red onion, hot pepper, and cilantro, or as a yogurt and cucumber salad with a spice rub. Leave the skin on the cucumber and run it through a juicer for a refreshing summer drink.

Store and Preserve: Sometimes the cucumber crop can get a bit out of control (heavy yielding). We like to throw the extra-large cucumbers into a juicer and harvest the extra-small ones to make pickles.

DILL

An annual herb in the same family as celery, dill's leaves and seeds are used as an herb and spice flavoring. The umbrella-shaped "umbels" of the dill plant are a pretty addition to the garden and, come pickling season, a helpful ingredient to have around en masse for your pickling pursuits.

Plant: Direct seed or transplant. If direct seeding, use row cover to aid in germination. We plant two distinct rows—one row for dill leaf harvest and one row for dill seed head harvest.

Common Pest(s): Aphids, slugs.

Harvest: Dill leaf can be harvested "cut and come again" style; alternatively, let the foliage grow until large dill heads form. Use a serrated knife and hold the top canopy of the greens in your hand while gently slicing the bottom of the plant about 1½ inches above the soil level. Leave enough stem so that the crop can regrow. To harvest dill seed heads, wait until the dill seed is of desired maturity and cut the stem below the dill seed head.

Enjoy: Mix the threadlike clusters of dill leaves with yogurt as a sauce. Garnish seafood, soups, potatoes, and vinegar with dill for a distinctively warm, slightly licorice flavor.

Store and Preserve: Store in the fridge, wrapped in a slightly damp paper towel. Fresh dill fronds can be frozen or dried.

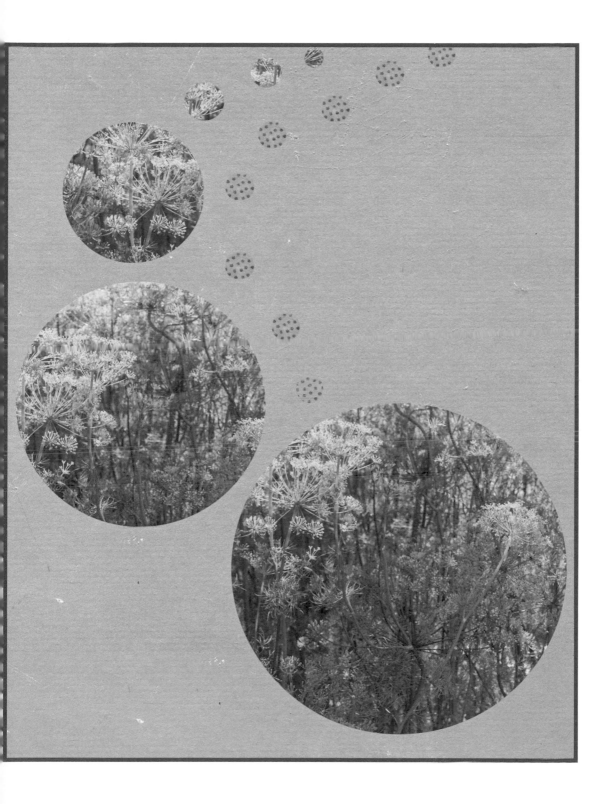

EDIBLE FLOWERS

Not only do edible flowers attract beneficial insects and pollinators to your garden, they spruce up any dish! The Willows loves them, and we grow quite a few. Some of our standbys are nasturtium, calendula, borage, marigolds, and bachelor's buttons.

Plant: Direct seed or transplant.

Enjoy: Nearly any dish is made more beautiful with the addition of edible flowers. Garnish soups, breads, salads, and cakes with their petals, or create flower-infused syrups for your next signature cocktail.

Store and Preserve: Once flowers are harvested, they should be used as quickly as possible. Instead of storing in a paper bag, which can crush their delicate petals, store edible flowers in a plastic container, on moist paper towels.

EGGPLANT

A tropical perennial that has been cultivated as an annual in temperate climates, the fruit of the eggplant, or "aubergine," is botanically classified as a berry. Like tomatoes, potatoes, and peppers, the eggplant is a species of nightshade grown for its fruit. There are a great number of eggplant cultivars beyond the most common bulbous, glossy purple variety usually displayed in stores. For something different than the grocery store standard, look for white eggplants; long, tapered Japanese eggplants; and tiny, egg-sized eggplants.

Plant: Eggplants are tricky when it comes to growing your own transplants. We recommend buying eggplant starts. Reusable weed barrier mulches help keep the warmth in and the weeds out. Eggplants are a great crop to grow in large containers or pots. They love a little shelter for warmth and disease protection, so if you have a greenhouse or similar space, invite your eggplants in. In lieu of a greenhouse, row cover supported with wire hoops works great as well. Planting varieties with different days to maturity will give you a long harvest with one planting.

Common Pest(s): Aphids, flea beetles.

Harvest: Expect to begin harvesting fully ripened fruit 60 to 70 days from the time of transplanting.

Enjoy: Ideal for Italian and Mediterranean recipes, eggplant can be roasted, grilled, or sautéed. The eggplant's meaty texture absorbs marinades well. Roast with peppers and zucchini and serve in a veggie sandwich with goat cheese, layer in lasagnas, add to Thai curries, or make a baba ganoush appetizer.

Store and Preserve: Store eggplant at room temperature, out of the sun. To freeze, slice eggplant and blanch in boiling water for four minutes. Cool and package in freezer bags. For dishes like eggplant parmesan, you can batter and bread eggplant slices after blanching, then wrap in wax paper and freeze.

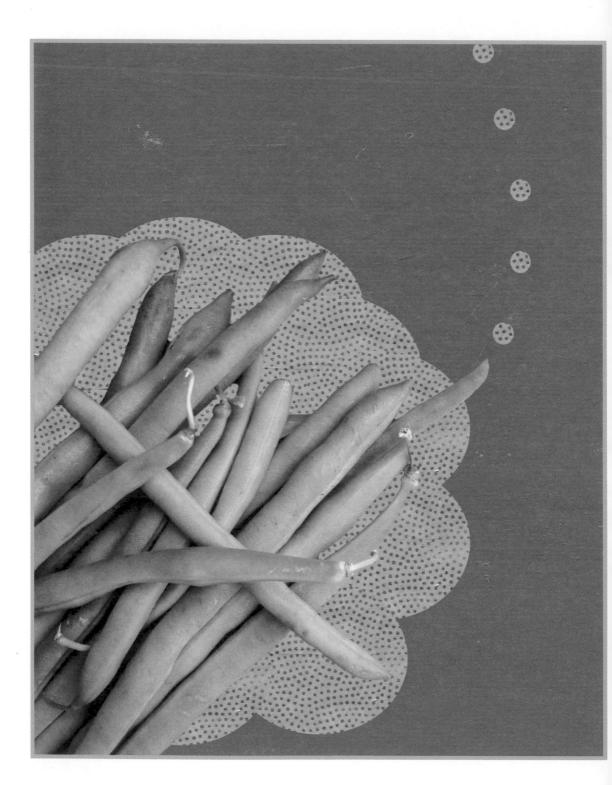

GREEN BEANS (BUSH AND POLE VARIETIES)

Green beans are classified into two main groups, bush and pole (vining) varieties. One of the most enjoyable harvests of the summer arrives when these tender beans are ready to be plucked. We snap beans and eat them right off the plant, or eat them lightly blanched and tossed with butter and a little salt. Because they're easy to grow and harvest, beans are a good fit for most any size garden and are especially fun for kids.

Plant: Direct seed or transplant. If direct seeding, use row cover to aid in germination and keep the birds from snacking on the tender shoots. Bush beans do not need trellising or additional support. Pole beans need support and prefer to have something to crawl up.

Harvest: Pick the tiny beans soon after they've formed, or wait a bit longer until they are full size. You'll know they are ready by the taste and texture. The size of the bean depends on the variety. Harvest pole beans when the pods begin to elongate, in 50 to 60 days. Harvest regularly to encourage new bean growth.

Enjoy: Few things taste more of summer than steamed green beans with butter and salt. For a spicier preparation, try Thai-style green beans with chile paste. Add your beans to a stir-fry or put them in a salad with tomatoes, feta, and herbs.

Store and Preserve: Trim the ends off the green beans, then cut them into desired lengths. Blanch in boiling water for two to four minutes, depending on the size of the bean. Plunge into a cold-water bath. Once cool, spread on a baking sheet and freeze until firm. Transfer to a freezer-safe container.

HEAD LETTUCE

This broad category of lettuces is an especially gratifying one to grow in the home garden due to the amazing variety of options available. From purple-flecked Troutback lettuce to dwarf romaines like Little Gem, there are plentiful colors and flavors of head lettuce to keep you in salads all summer long.

Plant: Transplant. Use row cover on young seedlings to protect from birds.

Common Pest(s): Slugs, birds.

Harvest: Get a double harvest by leaving 2 inches of the crop in the ground and harvesting the second cutting about two to three weeks later.

Enjoy: When summer comes around and the garden is at its height, it's easy to transition salads to center stage at the kitchen table. Create main course salads with the addition of other fresh veggies, unique grains, beans, olives, fruits, nuts, cheeses, meat, seafood, and a dressing of your own creation.

Store and Preserve: Wrap head lettuce in a paper towel, store in a plastic bag, and stick in the fridge.

HERBS: PERENNIAL FAVORITES

Sage, oregano, chives, thyme, rosemary, and mint are easy to grow and will bring your vegetables to life in the kitchen. Perennial herbs can be started from seed, but can often take longer to germinate and become established. You can buy or acquire seedlings or established herbs to transplant, for instant gratification. It is such a delight to be able to pluck a twig of oregano to add to spaghetti sauce, or some mint as an addition to a summer lemonade.

Plant: Transplant. Perennial herbs are great crops to plant into big pots or whisky barrel-type containers. When crop planning, remember that perennial herbs need space. Aim to give each herb seedling 2 feet to grow and spread. Research the growing patterns of each herb you plant, and take note of its growing habit. Does it grow upward and outward like a shrub, or is it a low-lying ground cover?

Harvest: When established, clip what you need with garden clippers or scissors. In the fall, cut the whole plant completely back to encourage new growth.

KALE

Toscano kale, also known as "lacinato" or "dinosaur" kale, is the backbone of one of the Willows Inn's most enduring and beloved snacks: a roasted kale leaf topped with a dollop of truffle puree. Packed with vitamins, kale is one of the most treasured vegetables on the farm due to its lengthy harvest window—it can be harvested throughout the Northwest winters if the season is mild. It has a substantial texture that holds its form well when added to stir-fries and sautés.

Plant: Direct seed or transplant. Use row cover to protect from pests. If cabbage moths are persistent, keep kale covered throughout the duration of the crop.

Common Pest(s): Imported cabbage moth, aphids, slugs, wireworms, birds.

Harvest: Begin harvesting kale as soon as the crop becomes established (this will look different depending on the variety). For large leaves of kale, expect to begin harvesting about 65 days after seeding. For baby leaves, begin harvesting about 30 days after seeding. At Loganita we leave the kale crop in the ground over winter with no frost protection and enjoy the flowering shoots the following spring.

Enjoy: Kale, like spinach, can easily be added to stir-fries, sautés, pastas, and soups for a nutritional and textural boost—white bean and kale soup or minestrone and kale soups are favorites. A simple raw kale salad can be made by finely chopping kale and massaging the chopped leaves with lemon juice. Or try making your own kale chips by drizzling with oil, salting, and baking in the oven. Remove the ribs of the kale before cooking.

Store and Preserve: Quickly blanch kale in boiling water for two minutes, then immediately submerge in a cold-water bath, dry, and freeze (freeze first on a cookie sheet, then put in an airtight container).

NAPA CABBAGE

A cool-season annual vegetable, the crinkly pale green leaves of the napa cabbage, a type of Chinese cabbage, are commonly used in Asian cuisine. Asian cabbages actually come from a different species than European cabbages. Thick ribs and soft outer leaves distinguish them from standard cabbages, and their flavor more closely resembles that of bok choy or broccoli raab. Chinese cabbage originated in China, but napa cabbage is thought to be a cross that occurred naturally between southern bok choy and northern turnips.

Plant: Transplant. Use row cover to protect from pests. If cabbage moths are persistent, keep the crop covered until harvest time. It is important to plant out napa cabbage after the risk of frost has passed. Young transplants are prone to bolting if exposed to frost.

Common Pest(s): Flea beetles, imported cabbage moths, birds.

Harvest: From the time of planting, expect full-size Chinese cabbage heads in 50 to 60 days. Harvesting Chinese cabbage early will result in smaller, loosely formed heads.

Enjoy: Make kimchi or shred and make into an Asian slaw. Napa cabbage is an ideal filling for dumplings or spring rolls, and can be shredded and added to soups and stir-fries (its ribs ensure it won't turn to mush).

Store and Preserve: Napa cabbage won't fit into most ziplock bags, so try using plastic wrap for storage in the fridge instead. Or shred and put in a ziplock bag. Napa cabbage can also be fermented into kimchi or sauerkraut.

ONIONS

Several years ago, the chefs asked me to grow the "cipollini" variety of onion. After tasting the dish they came up with, I knew exactly why they chose this onion! Cipollinis have more residual sugar than the average onion, making them a perfect candidate for roasting or caramelizing. These little onions are a great onion option for the small-scale, backyard grower because they are small and quick to mature.

Plant: Transplant. For late-maturing varieties, you'll have time for just one planting. For earlier-maturing varieties, plant two times, spacing the plantings one month apart.

Harvest: Depending on the variety, expect to harvest anywhere from 60 to 100 days from the time of seeding.

Enjoy: While onions are generally a component of recipes rather than their own dish, sweet onion varieties are absolutely delicious charred on the grill and served on their own. Onion rings and classic French onion soup also feature this allium.

Store and Preserve: Keep onions in a cool, dark, dry area—not in the fridge or in plastic bags, which will shorten their shelf life. If freezing, chop onions and spread in a single layer on a baking sheet (cover with plastic wrap to contain the smell) until firm. Transfer to ziplock bags or a freezer safe container.

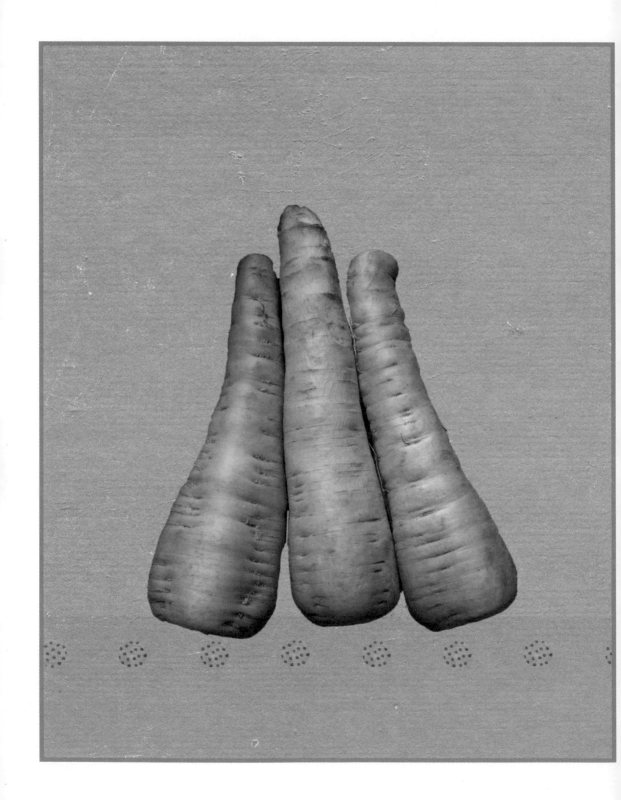

PARSNIPS

This tapered, cream-colored root vegetable is closely related to both carrots and parsley. Prior to the arrival of cane sugar to Europe, parsnips were used as a sweetener. They become sweeter as they endure winter frosts and the longer they are left in the ground.

Plant: Direct seed. Use row cover to aid in germination. Keep in mind that parsnips take up to three weeks to germinate.

Common Pest(s): Wireworms.

Harvest: Expect to harvest mature parsnips about four months after seeding. For big, mature parsnips ready to harvest in mid-October and beyond, seed no later than early April. Parsnips will hold in the ground during the harshest winter, and they will also hold for quite some time in a root cellar or refrigerator. Parsnips get sweeter with a frost!

Enjoy: Roast or glaze parsnips with other root vegetables for a warming winter vegetable dish. Mash parsnips with equal amounts of potatoes and a little cream, butter, and salt, or make a parsnip puree soup. If you're feeling adventurous, find a dessert recipe—parsnips are especially wonderful when paired with maple syrup.

Store and Preserve: Parsnips wrapped in a paper towel and stored in a plastic bag in the fridge will last a few weeks. For longer storage, cut parsnips into cubes and blanch for three minutes before plunging into a water bath, drying, and freezing.

PEAS: SUGAR SNAP AND SNOW

A new variety of pea was born in 1952 with the creation of the sugar snap pea, a sweet cross-breeding of the snow pea with a mutant shell pea. Both the crunchy, fuller sugar snap pea and the flatter snow pea can be eaten straight off the vine and are popular picks in kids' gardens. Don't forget to add the tender pea tendrils and flowers to your salad for the most delicate and tasty garnish.

Plant: Direct seed or transplant. Use row cover to prevent birds from snacking on the young seedlings and shoots. Some edible pea pod varieties grow tall and need additional support, like a trellis. Typically, one planting in the spring is sufficient and, if kept well-picked to encourage new growth, will produce well through July. Edible pod peas are also an excellent fall crop—plant your seeds in mid-July to get peas in late September.

Harvest: Start harvesting edible pod peas when the pods begin to mature. For an extra-tiny, delicate pea, try harvesting when the pod is just 1½ inches long. For a more full-size pea, wait until the pod is 2 to 3 inches long. Harvest regularly to encourage new pea pod growth.

Enjoy: Deliciously sweet fresh off the vine, whole pea pods shine when sautéed in a bit of olive oil with a pinch of salt. Toss into stir-fries and Asian noodle salads with other veggies, sesame oil, and soy sauce. You can also shell snap peas and use the fresh peas in a wide variety of dishes, from creamy risotto to pasta primavera to gnocchi.

Store and Preserve: To freeze snow peas and snap peas, blanch in boiling water for one to two minutes, then plunge into an ice bath for a few minutes. Remove, dry, and spread on a baking sheet and put in the freezer. Once hardened, transfer to a freezer-safe container.

PEPPERS: HOT AND SWEET

I used to think that peppers were a space-taker-upper and not worth the precious real estate in small gardens. Then I discovered the shisito and padrone varieties (thanks, chefs!) and am continually amazed by how many peppers a small, compact bush can produce. We fill up one of our greenhouses with both these varieties and pick peppers well into October.

Plant: Peppers are a great crop to grow in large containers or pots. Buy pepper plants from your favorite garden store or farmers' market stand, then transplant to the garden. Reusable weed barrier mulches help raise the soil temperature and keep out weeds. Like tomatoes, peppers thrive in warmth and are less susceptible to disease if they're given greenhouse space or grown under row cover supported by wire hoops. Spread your pepper harvest out by planting a few varieties that have different days to maturity.

Common Pest(s): Aphids, flea beetles.

Harvest: You should have fully ripened fruit 60 to 95 days from the time of transplanting.

POTATOES

Buttery and tender, freshly harvested potatoes are a treat! One of our favorites is the Makah Ozetteo, an heirloom potato that the Makah Nation named after one of their villages located around the coastal town of Neah Bay, Washington. Before becoming a home garden staple in Neah Bay, this unique fingerling-style potato was brought to Neah Bay from South America via Spanish conquests. After a hard winter, the Spanish abandoned their fort and the gardens within it, leaving the potatoes behind. The Makah continued the harvest, and so we continue to enjoy this potato today.

Plant: Cut up purchased seed potatoes, or use potatoes that you've saved from the previous year. Just make sure each piece has an "eye." When planting, keep the "eye" facing up. Frost can kill potato seedlings, so be sure to wait to plant until after any danger of frost has passed. If you must plant before the last frost date, use row cover for frost protection. Plant potatoes no later than June 1 to allow enough time for tubers to mature. Hilling potatoes helps keep weed pressure down around the plants and also encourages tuber growth. For in-ground plots: pile up soil around the foliage, making sure to leave a few inches of green stem sticking out. For raised bed plots (or closely planted rows in in-ground plots): pile up straw around the base of the plants, making sure to leave a few inches of green sticking out.

Common Pest(s): Wireworms.

Harvest: Begin harvesting baby potatoes after the plants have flowered. Harvest trick for early potatoes: instead of pulling out the entire plant, gently dig beneath the plant and harvest a few young tubers, leaving others to mature into larger potatoes. Alternatively, wait until the tubers are mature and harvest entire plants in early fall after the foliage has died off. Make sure to thoroughly dig around the perimeter of the plant—there might be more potatoes than you think!

Enjoy: One of the most versatile vegetables you can grow, there are few things more delicious than a freshly harvested potato, baked or boiled, and slathered with butter. For roasting in aluminum foil on the barbecue or on a cookie sheet or pan in the oven, cut potatoes into chunks or strips, toss with olive oil, throw in a little salt, pepper, rosemary, lemon juice, and garlic. Pureed potato-garlic soups are delicious, as are more modern renditions of the classic potato salad. Try skillet potatoes for breakfast, or grate and use as a hash or for latkes.

Store and Preserve: Store potatoes in a cool, dark place. If potatoes are stored in temperatures much below 50 degrees (for example, in the refrigerator), their starch is prone to turn to sugar, which changes the flavor and causes discoloration when cooked. Put potatoes in a breathable container such as a cardboard box or mesh bag to ensure good ventilation, and be sure to remove any potatoes that sprout or shrivel.

RADISHES

A staple on the breakfast menu at the Willows is the French Breakfast radish. It arrives in the Willows kitchen in plastic tubs, ready to be trimmed and groomed by the chefs exactly three weeks after the seed hits the soil. Because of how quickly they mature, radishes are an easy pick for kids' gardens. They'll be one of the very first things you get to pull out of the garden in early spring.

Plant: Direct seed. Use row cover to aid in germination and protect from pests.

Common Pests: Flea beetles, wireworms, birds, slugs.

Harvest: Begin harvesting radishes as soon as the roots begin to swell, or wait until they are a bit larger. It takes about 25 days for quick-growing radish varieties to reach the size of a quarter.

Enjoy: Thinly slice crunchy medallions of radish onto a sandwich or salad for a spicy flavor addition, or vinegar-brine for a quick garnish on tacos or burgers. If you have a bumper crop of radishes, make a batch of kimchi!

Store and Preserve: Radishes can be quick-pickled, fermented, or canned in a hot-water bath and stored.

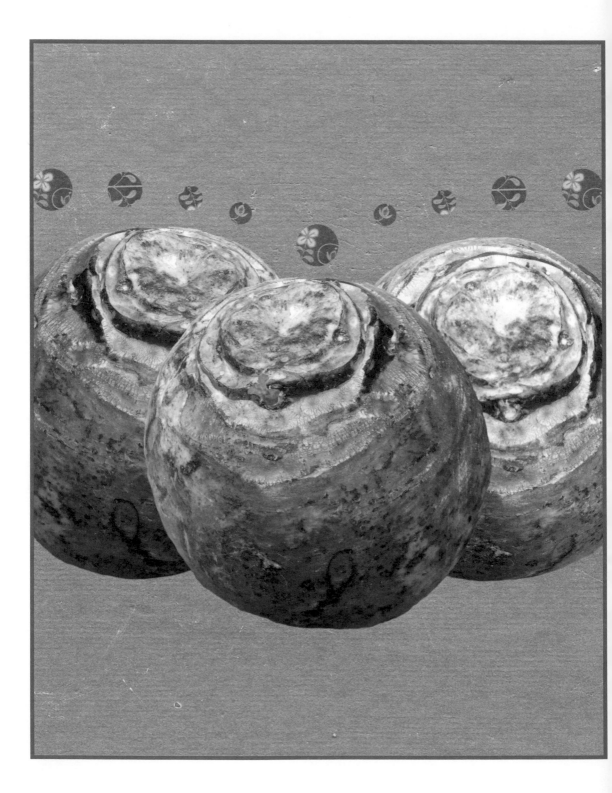

RUTABAGAS

A cross between a cabbage and a turnip, the humble rutabaga is often overlooked or thought of as a last-resort food due to its association with food shortages in World Wars I and II. We see the mildly sweet rutabaga differently! In its raw form, it has a mild flavor that is slightly tamer than that of turnips. But this root vegetable really shines in stews and casseroles. Sweet, savory, and rich all at once, it's a wonderfully satisfying addition to a winter meal. We harvest the large, plump rutabaga roots when they are at their finest in November and carefully store them. Come March, when the restaurant opens, they are featured on the early spring menu.

Plant: Typically, rutabagas are grown to be harvested in the fall. For big, mature rutabagas ready to harvest in mid-October and beyond, direct seed no later than mid-July. Use row cover to aid in germination and protect from pests.

Common Pest(s): Flea beetles, wireworms, birds, slugs.

Harvest: Expect to harvest mature rutabagas about three months after seeding.

Enjoy: Peel rutabagas prior to cooking. We like to mix rutabagas with carrots or potatoes in a mash or puree, adding a little cream and butter as we go. Add rutabagas to stews, or make a pureed soup. Because the flavor of the rutabaga is quite mild, you may want to add something with a bit of kick, like chile peppers or garlic.

Store and Preserve: In a cool root cellar, rutabagas will keep for several months if placed in sand or straw and covered with burlap bags (also filled with sand or straw). Air circulation is important for rutabaga longevity, so be sure to leave a little space between each one. Better yet, keep them in the ground until ready to use. For longer storage, peel and dice rutabagas, then blanch and freeze.

SALAD MIX

Leaf lettuce and mesclun are great "cut and come again" mixes that will keep you in salad from early spring through the fall.

Plant: Direct seed. Use row cover to aid in germination and protect from pests. Lettuce is cold hardy and will survive a light spring frost.

Common Pest(s): Slugs, birds.

Harvest: Begin harvesting the baby greens as soon as the crop has become established, when they are about 4 inches tall. Using a serrated knife, hold the top canopy of the greens in your hand while gently slicing the bottom of the plant about 1½ inches above the soil level. Make sure to leave enough stem so that the crop can regrow. Harvest greens in this manner no matter how tall they get. You will get better regrowth by making a clean cut near the bottom of the plants. You can expect a few cuttings, depending on your crop. After that, you'll notice the greens becoming tough and bitter.

Enjoy: Salad mix is best cut fresh from the garden as a side salad or as the base for a larger salad. Try making an entree out of salad greens, adding other garden veggies, olives or cheese, and a piece of fish, chicken, or beef.

Store and Preserve: After cutting salad greens, wash and dry, then place in a plastic bag with a layer of paper towels to soak up any remaining moisture. Refrigerate.

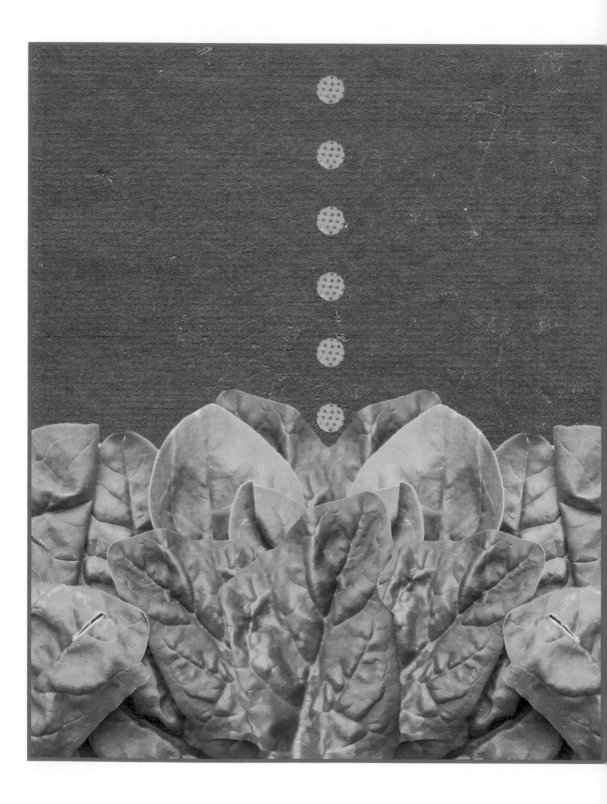

SPINACH

Originating in ancient Persia, this nutritional powerhouse is high in iron—ounce for ounce, it's higher than the same amount of beef. Spinach is also among the most pesticide-laden produce available, making it an ideal crop to grow organically in your culinary garden.

Plant: Direct seed. Use row cover to aid in germination and protect from pests.

Common Pest(s): Leaf miners, slugs, birds.

Harvest: For salad mix, begin harvesting the baby greens as soon as the crop has become established, when they are about 4 inches tall. We typically begin harvesting baby spinach three to four weeks from the time of seeding. If your end goal is larger spinach for cooking, simply let the greens get bigger. Using a serrated knife, hold the top canopy of the greens in your hand while gently slicing the bottom of the plant about 1½ inches above the soil level. Make sure to leave enough stem so that the crop can regrow. You will get better regrowth by making a clean cut near the bottom of the plants. Alternatively, clip individual spinach leaves from the outside of the plant. Expect two to three good harvests. After that, you'll notice the greens becoming tough and bitter. Spinach tends to bolt quickly.

Enjoy: Spinach salad is a favorite of ours, and a no-fuss way to enjoy spinach right out of the garden. Like kale, spinach is an easy ingredient to throw into stir-fries and soups at the last minute for a little extra color and nutrition. Add chopped spinach to smoothies for a quick nutritional boost.

Store and Preserve: Wrap spinach in paper towels to help absorb excess moisture before storing in a container in the fridge. Blanch spinach in boiling water for a minute, squeeze out excess moisture, chop, and freeze. Or puree spinach with a small amount of water and freeze in ice cube trays before tossing into a freezer bag.

SUMMER SQUASH

Summer squash is so called because, unlike the long-lasting, storable winter squash, this is squash that is best enjoyed in the summer. Famous examples include zucchini (also called courgette) and yellow squash. In the height of its season, summer squash is extremely prolific. Even though summer squash has an upright and compact growing habit, the leaves are huge and take up lots of space. In small-scale home gardens, summer squash is the perfect crop to plant on the edge of a bed, so it can spill out onto the pathway, saving precious garden space. The chefs have had me grow a lot of different kinds of zucchini and summer squash, but they keep coming back to the Italian heirloom variety Costata Romanesco. Not only does the flavor impress, but the Costatas produce many blossoms, a chef's delight.

Plant: Direct seed or transplant. Covering the soil with a reusable weed barrier and using row cover will help keep the plants cozy, especially during a cold and wet Pacific Northwest spring. For kitchen gardens, we suggest you look for varieties with ultra-compact growth habits. Remove the row cover as soon as the plants begin to flower, to allow for sufficient pollination.

Common Pest(s): Root maggots, slugs, birds.

Harvest: Expect to harvest the first baby summer squash fruit 50 days from the time of seeding. Harvest often to encourage growth.

Enjoy: Bake with a sprinkling of Parmesan cheese or sauté in a pan with a hearty tomato sauce and creamy polenta. Many summer squashes are good candidates for dessert and make great quick breads and cakes.

Store and Preserve: Keep squash dry for refrigerator storage instead of washing beforehand. Because they tend to grow in abundance, summer squash is ideal for canning, and makes a tasty snack when dried. To freeze, trim the ends and grate, or cut into cubes or slices (no need to peel). Blanch in boiling water for two to six minutes, depending on the size of the cut. Plunge into an ice-water bath and, once cool, freeze in a single layer on baking sheets before transferring to ziplock bags or a freezer-safe container.

SWISS CHARD

This voluptuous leafy green is high in vitamins, and the rainbow varieties bring a bold spectrum of color to the garden and plate. In contrast to what its name suggests, chard originated in the Mediterranean, not Switzerland. Swiss chard offers a continuous harvest throughout the summer and into early winter, with a texture that lands between spinach and kale. Like spinach and kale, it can easily be added to dishes for a quick nutritional boost.

Plant: Start seeds or transplant. If direct seeding, use row cover to aid in germination. If leaf miners are a threat, keep covered for the duration of the crop.

Common Pest(s): Leaf miners, slugs.

Harvest: For baby leaves, begin harvesting Swiss chard in 30 days from seeding. Pick outer leaves as needed, or harvest with a serrated knife as you would a "cut and come again" crop. Full-size outer leaves will be harvestable about 60 days from the time of seeding.

Enjoy: Of all the garden vegetables, Swiss chard seems to be the most perplexing to people when it comes to how best to use it. In reality, this Mediterranean cooking star has loads of uses in the kitchen. Delicious sautéed with a little garlic and olive oil, it can be used in most any dish that calls for kale or spinach. Try it in a creamy pasta with bacon and white sauce or finely shred into a wintry salad with roasted vegetables and a tangy dressing. Add to soups, stratas, and quiches for a vibrant burst of color.

Store and Preserve: If refrigerating, chard does better if left unwashed until ready to use. Blanch chard stems for two minutes or leaves for one minute in boiling water, then plunge into an ice-water bath before drying and freezing.

TOMATOES

Garden-fresh tomatoes are one of summer's most luscious offerings, and there are loads of varieties to choose from. Roma tomatoes are ideal sauce tomatoes for canning, cherry tomatoes absolutely burst with flavor, and colorful heirloom tomatoes are some of the season's true beauties. Because tomatoes thrive in hot environments, we grow them in our greenhouses. While I used to think a greenhouse was required to grow tomatoes, I was proved wrong by a farmer friend of mine who grows tomatoes in her sunny backyard quite successfully in large pots filled with potting soil.

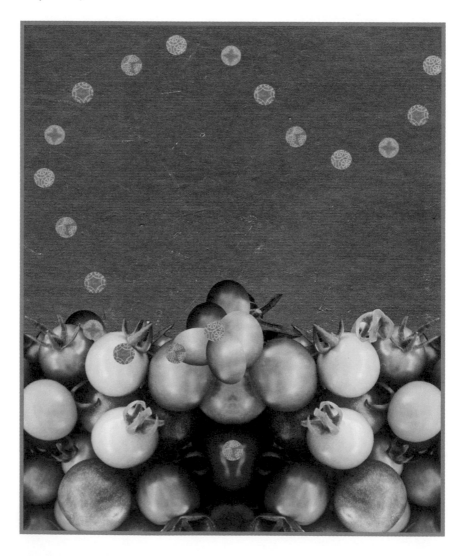

Plant: Unless you have a greenhouse setup or grow-lights, we recommend purchasing tomato plants from your favorite garden store or farmers' market stand. Reusable weed barrier mulches help raise the soil temperature (and keep out weeds).

Tomatoes benefit from regular pruning. At Loganita we prune each plant to two stems and remove the side shoots (also known as "suckers") once a week. When our tomato transplants are well established and they enter their fast and furious growth spurt, we attach twine to overhead supports and pull the twine to the base of the plant. The twine is then attached to the plant with tomato clips. Every week, we "string up" the growing plants by twisting the twine around the stem. All tomatoes benefit from a support system, whether it's a tomato cage, an overhead support system like ours, or just tying the plant to a single stake.

Common Pest(s): Aphids.

Harvest: A fully ripe tomato will easily separate from the vine. Green tomatoes can be harvested and then ripened indoors or, famously, fried and eaten straightaway.

Enjoy: There is no end to the tomato's usefulness in the kitchen, and a flavorful tomato is at its most elegant with a drizzle of quality olive oil and some nice salt. Combine with basil and mozzarella for a classic salad, or make a chunky salsa or a savory sauce for pasta. Nothing beats a tomato sandwich made with mayo and good bread.

Store and Preserve: Perfectly ripe tomatoes should be kept at room temperature, away from sunlight. If tomatoes are still ripening (or green), place them stem-side down in a single layer in a cardboard box or paper bag to assist with the ripening process. Tomatoes can be frozen whole, sliced, chopped, or pureed. To freeze whole tomatoes with skins on, simply cut away the stem scar, then set on a baking tray and freeze before transferring to a ziplock bag or freezer-safe container. If you prefer to freeze peeled tomatoes, remove the stem scar, then blanch in boiling water for one to two minutes. Peel and freeze as described previously. Tomatoes are great candidates for canning and drying as well.

TURNIPS: GLOBE

This traditional purple-top turnip is a classic fall crop that is sown in late July to be harvested in late September and October. In addition to the root, you can enjoy turnip-top greens.

Plant: Direct seed. Use row cover to aid in germination and protect from pests.

Common Pest(s): Flea beetles, wireworms, slugs, birds.

Harvest: Begin harvesting globe turnips as soon as the roots begin to swell, or wait until they are a bit larger. They reach their full size from about 50 days after direct seeding. Turnip thinnings are a great addition to your stir-fry!

Enjoy: Turnip greens make a delectable Southern-style sauté, especially when cooked with bacon or pork belly. Roast turnip roots on their own or with other root vegetables in olive oil, salt, and pepper, or make a creamy turnip and leek soup.

Store and Preserve: Once you harvest turnips, immediately cut off the tops to keep them from pulling moisture from the roots. Turnips can be stored in the refrigerator for two to three weeks. Freeze turnip roots by washing, peeling, and cutting them into cubes, then blanch in boiling water for two minutes. Plunge into a cold-water bath and freeze. Globe turnips will hold in the ground during a typical Pacific Northwest winter, and they will also hold for quite some time in the root cellar or refrigerator.

TURNIPS: SALAD

If your garden got started a bit late, these sweet, mild gems are a great choice because they mature in around just 30 days. A typical item on the spring menu at the Willows, the chefs love these delicate turnips and often serve them with the tender green leaves attached.

Plant: Direct seed. Use row cover to aid in germination and protect from pests. Don't plan on salad turnips holding well once the frost hits.

Common Pest(s): Flea beetles, wireworms, slugs, birds.

Harvest: Begin harvesting salad turnips as soon as the roots begin to swell, or wait until they are a bit larger. It takes about 35 days for golf-ball-sized salad turnips.

Enjoy: The flavor of these salad turnips is a little spicy, and they're delicious paired with a sweet apple in a raw winter salad or sautéed in olive oil with a little salt and pepper and a dash of vinegar.

Store and Preserve: Salad turnips can be quick-pickled, fermented, or canned in a hot-water bath and stored.

WINTER SQUASH

Winter squash has a hard rind and, unlike summer squash, is harvested when the seeds have fully matured. It takes up a fair amount of space in the garden, so give its vines space to wander. Winter squash stores extremely well and offers a gorgeous array of colors, textures, and unusual shapes to choose from. Doing what they do best, the chefs have narrowed down a few varieties that they deem to have the best flavor. The Cinderella pumpkin and Sweet Meat squash make the crop list every year, along with other varieties we trial for flavor and storability.

Plant: Direct seed or transplant out. Covering the soil with reusable weed barrier and the crop with row cover will help keep the plants cozy. Remove row cover as soon as the plants begin to flower, to allow for sufficient pollination.

Common Pest(s): Root maggots, slugs, birds.

Harvest: Make certain to harvest before a hard frost. Some varieties improve in flavor after storing for a month or more. Be sure to check for specific harvest and/or storage instructions for each unique variety.

Enjoy: Roast winter squash whole or cubed. A natural addition to warming dishes like risotto, lentils, or wild rice, winter squash soup can hold its own with a variety of flavor profiles, from Indian to Italian. Winter squash desserts like quick breads and cakes are dense, moist, and delicious.

Store and Preserve: If storing for winter, cure in the sun for 7 to 10 days and wipe down with a 1:4 part vinegar:water solution. Pack loosely in newspaper and store in open cardboard boxes or another container that will allow for air circulation. Squash stores best at around 55 degrees (not colder than 50 degrees), but can also keep for a few months in higher temperatures. It prefers a cool, dark place with about 60 percent humidity. To freeze, cut into cubes and lay in a single layer on a baking sheet until frozen, then transfer into ziplock bags or freezer-safe containers. Alternatively, roast or bake the squash. Remove the skin and mash. Once cool, transfer to the freezer.

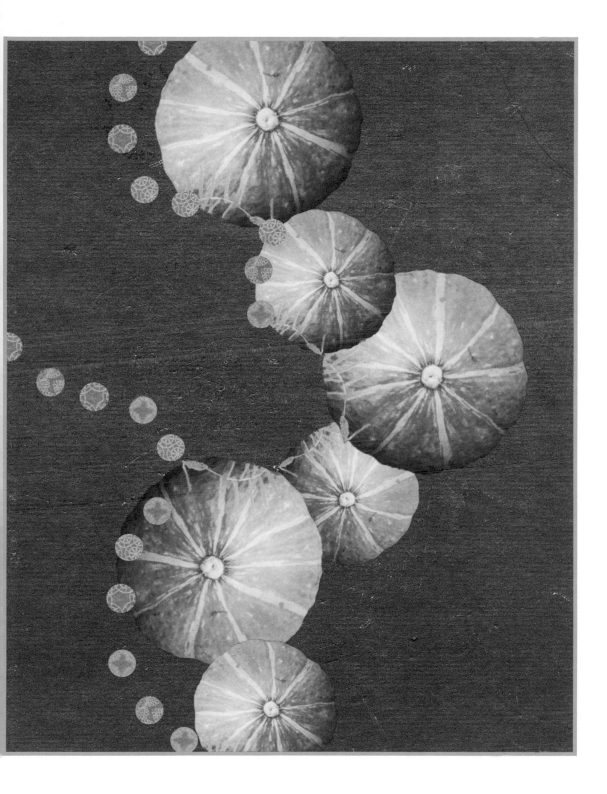

THE WILLOWS INN—
SPECIAL REQUESTS

Blaine and I are constantly experimenting with new plants and new varieties. Here are some veggies I'd never worked with before Blaine and I started collaborating on expanding what our culinary garden could be.

CELTUCE

Nobody quite knows what to make of the celtuce when they see it in the field. It looks like a lettuce plant that has been left far too long in the ground. Both the leaves and the long, thick stem are edible. I was lucky enough to be in the kitchen when the chefs were experimenting with a celtuce dish and got to experience the rich, nutty flavor of this unique vegetable. Now I know what the fuss is all about!

LAND SEAWEED, OR OKAHIJIKI

Land seaweed caught my eye in a seed catalog, and I thought it would be right up the chef's alley. I was right! Its delicate, succulent leaves that are loaded with vitamins and minerals have made their way to the menu atop the Herbed Tostada.

LOVAGE

Lovage is a relative of celery, carrots, and parsley, and we harvest this aromatic perennial herb by the bushel. The chefs use the stem, leaves, and the young flower tops to make an infused oil that is a key companion to their seafood-based dishes.

OYSTER LEAF

It took me a few years of failed attempts to get the oyster leaf seeds to germinate. When I finally delivered the first harvest of this crop, I was just as excited to be able to grow it as the chefs were to be able to add it to the menu. The delicate, fleshy leaves have a flavor reminiscent of oysters and are a must-have in the chef's garden.

SHISO

Early on in my culinary career, I was asked to grow shiso. I had never heard of it and was eager to give it a go. The pungent flavors of cinnamon, mint, basil, and anise are a chef's dream. The prolific and easygoing growing habit are a farmer's dream. Shiso has made its way into a variety of dishes and late-night chef's projects at the Willows, but holds its permanent place on the cocktail menu.

SUCCULENT ICE PLANT

In one of our planning meetings, Blaine requested that I grow ice plant, which is both sparkly and juicy. I got right to work researching growing habits and seed sources. As promised, I delivered our trial run of ice plant as soon as it became harvestable that season. The chefs fell in love with the meaty stems and leaves, which are covered in little water-filled bladder cells, giving the plant its sparkling appearance.

Asking advice from seasoned growers has always been, and continues to be, my practice when I have a gardening question. I also scour the Internet and read books, but it's the words from other farmers that really stick. I remember driving, in my early farming years, half an hour with a freshly picked delicata squash to ask a farmer friend if the squash was fully ripe or not. He took one look and, pointing at the colored ridges on the squash, said, "It's not ripe until the stripes are as bright as the sunset." To this day, I say these words in my head when inspecting delicata for ripeness.

It isn't ripe until the stripes are as bright as a sunset.

You may want to take measures to protect your garden

AN INDEX OF PESTS AND HOW TO MANAGE THEM

It's easier to prevent pests from establishing themselves in the garden than it is to react to them once they're already there. Plants are like our human bodies in that we are all more vulnerable when we're stressed. Keeping the whole system of your garden healthy is the best protection against pest problems.

Establishing a few key practices in the garden will ensure that your seedlings have the best possible start to a healthy life. Maintaining soil health, staying on top of weeds, and checking plants regularly for pests will be your best upfront defense against problems.

There are plenty of creative solutions for keeping pests at bay once they've entered the garden. Your county extension, local gardening store, and experienced farmer or gardener friends are great resources for pest management.

APHIDS

These tiny, oblong critters are wingless and appear in multiple colors, from white to gray to black. They also tend to multiply quickly and appear in colonies as they suck the sap from your plants, causing wilting and yellowing, so it's best to catch them before they arrive en masse. The good news is that they are slow moving, so they are relatively easy to catch.

Solutions: If aphids appear on a strong, established crop like kale or cabbage (a few of their favorites), squirt a high-powered hose right at them to drown them and get them off the leaves. For less sturdy plants, try an organic aphid spray, neem oil, a homemade spray like dish soap and water, or ladybugs. To get aphids off a harvested crop, soak the plant in saltwater. The aphids will rise to the surface and abandon the plant.

BIRDS

Birds can be helpful in the garden, as they eat insects, grubs, caterpillars, and mice, but if they're also eating seeds and germinated sprouts, you may want to take measures to protect your garden.

Solution: Use row cover or overhead netting on your garden beds, especially over newly established plants.

CABBAGE MOTHS/WORMS

These slow-moving green larvae love to munch on cabbage and other brassica family crops. Adults develop into white- or pale yellow–winged butterflies. They're especially damaging later in the growing season and, depending on their growth stage, will leave translucent scars or chew irregular holes as they bore into plants.

Solutions: Use row cover to act as a physical barrier against cabbage moths. If visible, pluck them off immediately.

DEER

With an impressive ability for leaping, deer can do some serious damage to vegetation and trees if left to roam free. In the garden, their presence is often made known by the jagged cuts they make with their teeth and the hoof marks left in your garden.

Solution: Install fencing that is 8 to 10 feet high, or two 4-foot fences, spaced 3 feet apart. (Deer can jump high and wide, but can't do both simultaneously.) Put netting or hoops over raised beds.

FLEA BEETLES

Flea beetles jump like fleas but look like beetles, and tend to leap away when approached. They make holes in leaves, especially in new seedlings. They don't tend to kill mature plants, but do spread blight and wilt, so you should eradicate them as soon as possible.

Solutions: Row cover is a good preventative measure. To control flea beetles, try neem oil, an OMRI-certified flea beetle spray.

LEAF MINERS

You'll recognize leaf miner damage by the squiggly-lined trail they bite through leaves. A leaf miner is the larva of an insect—usually a moth or fly—that lives between the upper and lower surfaces of leaves.

Solutions: At the first sign of their presence in leaves, squeeze the larvae in the leaves between your fingers to kill them or remove the entire leaf, if damage is extensive, to prevent further spreading. Row cover helps prevent flies from lighting on leaves, and neem oil is a natural repellent.

RABBITS

With a reputation for multiplication and a penchant for vegetables, rabbits are a burrowing pest you'll want to keep out of the garden. Signs of a rabbit problem include clean-cut vegetable damage at the base of plants, especially in the plants' young stages. Rabbits tend to burrow, and holes can be an indicator of their presence in your garden.

Solution: Protect individual raised beds with hoops and chicken wire. In the early spring, install a chicken-wire fence that is 4 feet high and buried 6 inches deep in the ground.

ROOT MAGGOTS

Adult root maggots look like small gray-black flies. They lay their eggs at the base of plants, in the soil. Larvae feed on young roots and germinating seeds, and then the cycle begins again. Plants with root maggot presence look rotten at their bases.

Solutions: Row cover is a good preventative for fresh seed beds, and a sprinkling of OMRI-certified diatomaceous earth around seedlings can help deter adults. Applying beneficial nematodes on top of the soil or around plants is helpful in getting rid of larvae.

SLUGS

A well-known pest of the Northwest garden, the mighty slug can do some serious damage in a night of eating. You'll know they've been by if you see a line of shimmering slime and their signature jagged bite on plants.

Solutions: Row cover helps create an obstacle for slugs, and OMRI-listed Sluggo is a good pick as a slug deterrent.

WIREWORMS

Tough, thin worms that are yellow to brown-red in color, wireworms feed underground, munching on germinating seeds, roots, and tubers. Resulting plants wilt and die.

Solutions: Because wireworms attack crops underground, constant cultivation (with a hula hoe) helps deter them. Once established, use potatoes or old cabbage stalks to trap them, then dispose. Wireworms like cooler temperatures and row cover helps heat up the soil, pushing them away.

THE NITTY-GRITTY

Quick and Dirty Greenhouse

For a simple low tunnel, purchase galvanized electrical tubing from your local hardware store and a "quick hoops bender" from Johnny's Selected Seeds catalog or a similar source to help you bend the tubing. Electrical tubing is sold in 10-foot lengths, which translates to be about a 4-foot high tunnel. Sink the hoops at least 8 inches deep in the soil, or until they feel secure, and place one hoop every 4 feet. Lay 6-mil greenhouse plastic over the top and secure with sandbags or weights. Your seedlings and demanding plants will be cozy and protected now. Just make sure it doesn't get too hot at summer's height!

Irrigation

While we are strong supporters of drip irrigation, there are places where each of the following systems makes sense.

	PROS	CONS
Drip irrigation	Consistent, can be timed, saves time, conserves water, puts water directly at the root system	Requires initial setup and hardware, potential leaks
Overhead/sprinkler	Instant, requires very little hardware, can be timed, covers large areas easily	Uses more water (much evaporates), nonspecific water stream, some crops don't like wet leaves, fungal disease
Hand-watering/wand	Forces you to look at plants as you water, easy hardware, focused water stream	Inconsistent, requires most time, some crops don't like wet leaves, fungal disease

Drip Irrigation

DRIP IRRIGATION SETUP 101: MARY'S TRIED-AND-TRUE DRIP IRRIGATION FORMULA USING DRIP TAPE:

Drip tape is a thin, flat, flexible plastic hose that delivers water to your crops via little slits that are evenly spaced. Designed for use with low water pressure, where the water flows slowly through the line and drips into the soil through the slits, drip tape runs down the length of your garden. First, though, you must get the water from your hose to the drip tape.

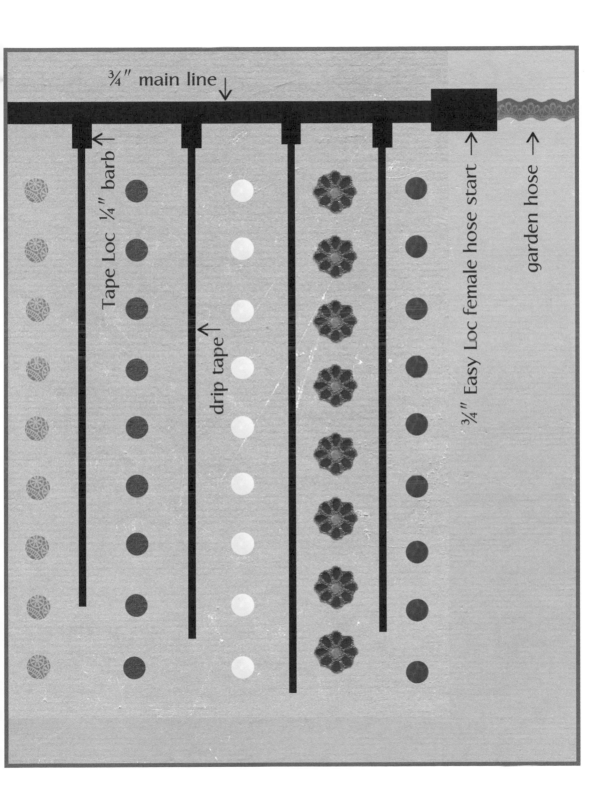

A dedicated **faucet** makes this whole project work, and then a **battery-operated timer** really makes it sing. A timer allows you to automate your watering times, which in turn frees up your time and ensures watering consistency. Attach a timer to your faucet.

Next, attach a 10-psi **pressure regulator** to the timer. A pressure regulator is a must-have, because drip tape isn't designed for use under full pressure. Without a pressure regulator, the high water pressure will cause the slits in the drip tape to burst open.

Connect a standard **garden hose** to the pressure regulator, then run the hose to your garden.

Next up: attaching the ¾-inch **polyethylene mainline tube** to the garden hose. Your ¾-inch mainline tube is what delivers water to your **T-tape**. Connect the ¾-inch mainline tube to the garden hose using a ¾-**inch Easy Loc female hose start**. Lay the ¾-inch mainline tube along the width of your garden bed. Don't forget to plug the end of the ¾-inch mainline with an **end cap**.

Punch holes into the ¾-inch mainline tube with a **punch tool**, and connect the drip tape to the ¾-inch mainline tube using a **Tape Loc ¼-inch barb**.

Lay the drip tape down the length of your garden bed directly after planting. It's a real pain to lay drip line after the crop has become established. For a 4-foot-wide bed, I typically use four drip tape lines spaced evenly apart to adequately water the bed. Seal off the ends of the drip tape by folding the end and slipping a piece of 6-inch drip tape over the folded end to stop the flow of water.

Accidentally slice your T-tape while harvesting? No problem—simply fix the leak with a **drip tape coupler**. Use landscape staples to hold the T-tape in place. If you are using well water, I recommend installing a **water filter** first (before the timer) to remove sand and silt.

Even if you have a drip irrigation system set up, always give freshly planted crops a good soak after you plant them. Direct seeded crops in raised beds dry out quickly and benefit from hand-watering as needed until they germinate. But don't worry, after germination the drip irrigation does its job.

A FEW GARDEN-FRESH RECIPES

Anne's Favorite Fresh Carrot Soup

With so few ingredients, the flavors and integrity of each ingredient shine. Tender garden carrots bring their wonderful sweet flavor. Grind the coriander by hand with a mortar and pestle, if possible, and use homemade chicken stock if you have it. If not, the grocery store variety will do just fine!

This soup creates the perfect spring meal, paired with some simple greens and toasted bread. I like to finish the soup with a little drizzle of reduced balsamic vinegar.

2 teaspoons olive oil

1 pound (about 2) yellow onions, peeled and thinly sliced

2 teaspoons whole coriander, ground with a mortar and pestle

2 pounds spring carrots, peeled and thinly sliced

6½ cups chicken stock

Heat the oil in a heavy-bottomed pan and cook the onions with the ground coriander over very low heat until translucent, 5 to 10 minutes. Add the carrots and stir to combine well. Pour in the chicken stock and bring to a boil. Reduce heat to a simmer for about 30 minutes, uncovered. Remove from heat and puree until smooth, using an immersion blender. Salt to taste.

Pesto!

This is my mother and grandmother's recipe for pesto. But, it is flexible. Some people use only basil, no parsley. Some people use almonds or walnuts instead of pine nuts. It all works out! You can even use carrot greens to make pesto.

½ cup fresh basil leaves	Add the first five ingredients to a food processor and puree. Add olive oil little by little until the pesto becomes a soft paste. Use fresh, refrigerate, or freeze.
½ cup fresh parsley	
½ cup grated parmesan	
⅓ cup pine nuts	
2 to 4 garlic cloves, minced	
¼ to ½ cup olive oil	

My mother used to make batches of pesto in the summer and freeze them in ice cube trays. She'd turn them out into plastic bags and store them in the freezer to use throughout the year. It's a way to taste July in midwinter.

The Willows' Potato Salad

FOR THE WALNUT DRESSING:

1⅓ cups walnuts

1¼ cups grape seed oil

4 teaspoons whole grain
　　mustard

⅓ cup white balsamic
　　vinegar

Salt

Pepper

FOR THE POTATOES:

1 pound potatoes,
　　mix of 5 varieties

1 apple

1 French Breakfast radish

1 watermelon radish

Herbs such as dill, sage,
　　oregano, and winter
　　savory to taste

Celery leaves to taste

Flaked sea salt to taste

Roast walnuts in 350°F oven for 10 to 12 minutes. Cool, reserve ⅓ cup, and roughly chop. Put all the oil and the cooled walnuts in a blender, and blend at high speed for 6 minutes. Strain and cool the oil completely. In a separate bowl, add the mustard, the vinegar, and 1 teaspoon of salt. Whisk. Then add the oil, slowly at first to form an emulsion, then more quickly as the dressing develops. Add pepper and adjust the seasonings.

Simmer the potatoes in water until tender. Blue potatoes take considerably longer. Drain the potatoes and let them cool.

TO ASSEMBLE THE SALAD:

Using a mandolin, slice the radishes very thin, and shave the apple twice as thick as the radish. Slice the cooked potatoes by hand at different thicknesses to showcase the variety. Place the potatoes around the bottom and sides of the serving bowl, alternating the different varieties. Then layer the radishes and apples, and a few more potato pieces on top of the base of potatoes. Spoon the dressing over the salad. Tear the herb leaves into small pieces and spread them over the top of the salad . Sprinkle the reserved chopped walnuts on top. Finish with the celery leaves, and season with flaked sea salt.

Mary's Hearty Greens Soufflé

In the late fall through early spring, the hearty greens stand tall at Loganita while everything else has been tucked away into cold storage and the root cellar. What I love most about this recipe is that you can use what you have. Grab a generous handful each of kale, Swiss chard, spinach, and collards or, alternatively, use just one kind of green. The hearty greens soufflé is an excellent way to use up excess greens while also getting a liberal dose of vitamins! When I was growing up, this was a standard on the dinner table, and I am excited to share my mom's recipe.

2 tablespoons butter

½ yellow onion, peeled and sliced

6 cups chopped and stemmed greens

1 cup chicken stock

Nutmeg

Salt and pepper

1 cup heavy cream

4 eggs

Heat the butter in a heavy-bottomed pan and sauté the onions and greens for 2 to 3 minutes. Add the chicken stock and cook uncovered for about 15 minutes, stirring every few minutes. Add a dash each of salt, pepper, and nutmeg. Transfer to a food processor, and add the heavy cream and eggs. Blend until smooth. Pour into a buttered casserole dish and bake at 350°F for about 45 minutes, or until set. Serves six.

The hearty greens soufflé makes the perfect side dish for a cozy, winter meal. In March, I always make a huge batch of soufflé with the overwintered greens I've cleared out to make room for the new spring seedlings.

The farmer's next year is always her best year.

Years ago, I heard an old-timer farmer say, "The farmer's best year is her next year." There is always a moment or two during farm season when I say to myself, "I'm doing this differently next year." The great thing about mistakes and mishaps on the farm is that they help me gain valuable knowledge and experience.

Every year, I'm looking at a new set of mistakes and mishaps, which will, in turn, make the next year the best year ever. It's a constant cycle of building knowledge and experience. This is one of my favorite parts about farming: always learning, always growing.

RESOURCES

I utilize a lot of seed companies and am always on the lookout for unique crops and seed companies I haven't stumbled across before. I encourage you to do the same! Here is a list of some of the go-to companies that we've used over the years.

Seeds:

Johnny's Selected Seeds (johnnyseeds.com; also a great resource for information on growing and supplies)

Territorial Seed Company (territorialseed.com)

Uprising Seeds (uprisingorganics.com)

Seeds of Change (seedsofchange.com)

Seeds from Italy (growitalian.com)

Trade Winds Fruit (tradewindsfruit.com)

Row 7 Seeds (row7seeds.com)

Seed Savers Exchange (seedsavers.org)

Baker Creek Heirloom Seeds (rareseeds.com)

Strictly Medicinal Seeds (strictlymedicinalseeds.com)

Wild Garden Seed (wildgardenseed.com)

Drip Irrigation Supplies:

DripWorks (www.dripworks.com)

Growing Supplies:

Your local farm and garden store!

Johnny's Selected Seeds (johnnyseeds.com)

Further Reading:

Chelsea Green Publishing (chelseagreen.com; a great, reliable source for excellent farm and gardening books)

Soil Testing:

Your local cooperative extension office

Willam F. Black Soil Testing (wfblacksoiltester.wixsite.com/soiltesting)

THE CHART OF ALL THINGS

	SP	IG	SUC	CH	CCA	DIRECT SEED/TRANSPLANT (RECOMMENDED)	SOW DEPTH	SEEDS PER INCH (PER CELL FOR TRANSPLANT CROPS)	DISTANCE BETWEEN EACH SEEDLING
Arugula		X	X	X	X	DS	½"	Steady sprinkle of seeds. About 60 seeds per foot.	n/a
Asian Greens		X	X	X	X	DS	½"	Steady sprinkle of seeds. About 60 seeds per foot.	n/a
Basil			X	X	X	T	¼"	3–6 per cell.	8" Do not thin the cell.
Beets			X	X		DS/T	½"	2 per inch; 2 per cell.	Thin to 2"
Bok Choy		X	X	X	X	T	½"	2 per cell.	6"
Broccoli			X	X		T	¼"	2 per cell.	12" Thin the cell to 1 seedling for a larger plant, or leave the 2 planted together for a smaller plant.
Cabbage			X			T	¼"	2 per cell.	12" Thin the cell to 1 seedling for a full-size cabbage, c leave the 2 planted together for 2 smaller cabbages.
Carrots			X	X		DS	½"	3–4 per inch.	Thin to 1"
Cauliflower			X			T	¼"	2 per cell.	12" Thin the cell to 1 seedling for a larger plant, or lea the 2 planted together for a smaller plant.
Celery			X	X	X	T	¼"	2 per cell.	8" Thin the cell to 1 seedling.
Cilantro			X			DS/T	½"	1 per inch; 4–6 per cell.	If transplanting, plant each cell 6" apart.
Cucumber			X	X		DS/T	1"	2 to 3 seeds planted together; 2 to 3 seed per cell.	12" Do not thin the cell. Plant each cell as 1 seedling.
Dill			X	X	X	DS/T	½"	Steady sprinkle of seeds; 4–6 seeds per cell.	No need to thin the cell. Transplant each cell 6" apart.
Edible Flowers						DS/T	½"	2–3 seeds planted together; 2–3 seeds per cell.	If transplanting, plant each cell 6" apart.
Eggplant	X			X		T	¼"	2 per cell.	12"
Green Beans: Bush			X	X		DS/T	1"	1 per inch; 4 per cell.	Do not thin the cell. If transplanting, plant each cell 8" apart.
Green Beans: Pole			X	X		DS/T	1"	4 seeds planted together; 4 seeds per cell.	Do not thin the cell. Plant each cell under the pole or stake which the plants will climb.
Head Lettuce			X	X	X	T	¼"	2 per cell.	8"
Herbs									
Kale			X	X	X	T	¼"	2 per cell.	12" Do not thin the cell.
Napa Cabbage			X			T	¼"	2 per cell.	12" Thin the cell to 1 plant.
Onion	X			X		T	¼"	2–3 per cell.	8" Do not thin the cell. Plant each cell as one seedlin
Parsnip	X			X		DS	½"	2–3 per inch	Thin to 3"
Peas: Snow			X	X		DS/T	1"	1 per inch; 4–6 per cell	Do not thin the cell. Plant each cell as 1 seedling. Plant each cell 6" apart.
Peas: Sugar Snap			X	X		DS/T	1"	1 per inch; 4–6 per cell.	Do not thin the cell. Plant each cell as 1 seedling. Plant each cell 6" apart.
Peppers: Hot, Sweet	X			X		T	¼"	1 seed per cell.	18"
Potatoes	X			X		DS	6"	1 seed potato per 8".	8"
Radish		X	X	X		DS	½"	2 per inch.	Thin to 1"
Rutabaga	X			X		DS	½"	2–3 per inch.	Thin to 4"
Salad Mix		X	X	X	X	DS	½"	Steady sprinkle. About 60 seeds per foot.	n/a
Spinach			X	X	X	DS/T	½"	2 per inch; 2 per cell.	Do not seed the cell. Plant each cell 6" apart.
Summer Squash			X	X		DS/T	1"	2 seeds every 24"; 2 seeds per cell.	24" If direct seeding, thin to 1 plant.
Swiss Chard			X	X	X	DS/T	¼"	1 seed per inch; 2 seeds per cell.	Don't thin the cell; plant each cell 12" apart. For a smaller leaf crop, direct seed and don't thin.
Tomatoes (Slicing and Cherry)	X			X		T	¼"	1 seed per cell.	24"
Turnip: Globe			X	X		DS	½"	2–3 per inch.	1"
Turnip: Salad		X	X	X		DS	½"	2–3 per inch	1"
Winter Squash	X					DS/T	¾"	2 per inch; 2 per cell.	24" For both direct seeding and transplanting, thin to 1 plant.

SP = Single Planting, IG = Instant Gratification, SUC = Succession Planting, CH = Continuous Harvest, CCA = Cut and Come Again

...CE IN ROWS	DAYS TO MATURITY	SPECIAL CONSIDERATIONS	SUCCESSION PLANTING SUGGESTIONS	FALL HARVEST SUGGESTIONS (NO GREENHOUSE REQUIRED, USE ROW COVER FOR ADDED PROTECTION)
	35–40	Spring and fall plantings only.	Seed every 2 weeks in spring.	Seed every 2 weeks mid-August through mid- to end of September.
	35–40		Direct seed every 2 to 3 weeks throughout growing season.	Seed final crop by mid- to end of September.
	40–80		3 plantings spaced 3 weeks apart will keep you in basil all summer long.	n/a
	55		Seed every 3 weeks throughout growing season.	Seed final crop by late July.
	40–50		Seed every 3 weeks throughout growing season.	Seed final crop by mid- to end of September.
	50–70		Once a month.	Transplant final crop by mid-July.
	65–85		Once a month.	Transplant final crop by mid-July.
	50–70		Every 3 weeks throughout growing season.	Seed final crop by late July.
	50–75		Once a month.	Transplant final crop by mid-July.
	80	Transplant out when nighttime temperatures are above 50°.	Once a month.	Transplant final crop by mid-July.
	50 for leaf harvest, 90–120 for seed harvest.		Seed every 2 to 3 weeks.	Seed final crop by early September.
	50		2 plantings, 1 month apart.	
	40–50 for leaf harvest; 80–100 for seed.		Seed every 3 weeks for continous leaf harvest.	Seed final crop by early September.
			2 plantings, 1 month apart.	
	60–70 days after transplanting.	Transplant out when nighttime temperatures are above 50°.		
	50–55	Transplant out when nighttime temperatures are above 50°.	3 plantings 3 weeks apart.	
poles, 24" apart ...ns to climb.	55–65	Transplant out when nighttime temperatures are above 50°.	2 plantings, 1 month apart.	
	45–55		Seed every 3 weeks for continuous harvest.	Transplant final crop by late August.
	30–65		2 plantings during main season, 1 planting for fall harvest.	Transplant final crop by mid-July.
	50–60		2 plantings during main season, 1 planting for fall harvest.	Transplant final crop by mid-July.
	60–100			
	120			Spring planted crop is to be harvested in the fall.
	60		1 spring planting and 1 fall planting.	Seed early July for fall harvest.
	50–65		1 spring planting and 1 fall planting.	Seed early July for fall harvest.
	60–95 days after transplanting.	Transplant out when nighttime temperatures are above 50°.		
	Variable, check variety.			
	25–35		Every 3 weeks throughout growing season for continuous harvest.	Seed final crop of standard radish varieties in late August. Seed fall varieties in mid- to late July.
	90–95		1 spring planting and 1 summer planting.	Seed final crop mid- to late July for fall.
	30		Every 2 weeks throughout growing season.	Seed final crop early September.
	35		Every 3 weeks for continuous harvest.	Seed final crop late August.
	50 days (both direct seeding and transplanting).	Transplant out when nighttime temperatures are above 50°.	2 plantings 1 month apart.	n/a
	30–60		1 spring planting and 1 summer planting.	Transplant in mid- to end of July for fall harvest.
	70 to 80 days after transplanting.	Transplant out when nighttime temperatures are above 50°.		n/a
	25–35		Every 4 weeks throughout growing season.	Seed final crop late July.
	25–35		Every 2 weeks throughout growing season.	Seed final crop early August.
	90–105 days (both direct seeding and transplanting).	Transplant out when nighttime temperatures are above 50°.		n/a

THE CHART OF ALL THINGS | 137

ACKNOWLEDGMENTS

Steve McMinn dreamed up the garden and is co-owner of Loganita Farms.

Kevin Burke helped Steve site and design the garden, and build necessary infrastructure (fences, greenhouses, raised beds, warming tables for seedlings, and the list goes on). Many thanks also to Blaine Wetzel, chef; Reid Johnson, manager; and the hardworking chefs and the entire team at the Willows Inn on Lummi Island.

Luna Perry has been a great help to Mary and companion to baby Trell during long summer gardening days. For advice, many thanks to Natasha Marin, and also to Uprising Seeds (Crystine Goldberg and Brian Campbell). For many of the photographs: Charity Burgraaf (check out her work at www.charitylynne.com and in Blaine's book *Sea and Smoke*). And, lovingly, thanks to our farm team: Chelsee Boucher, Shelli Thompson, and Katie Johnson.

Mary von Krusenstiern has been farming on small-scale, diversified organic vegetable operations since 2005, and in 2013 she became the founding culinary farmer at Loganita Farm. Her young son, Trell, often accompanies her on the farm. When not farming, Mary enjoys playing bluegrass music with her band and spending time in the outdoors in Glacier, Washington, where she lives. Mary also offers culinary gardening consulting services.

Anne Treat began writing articles about food and farming in 2004. Raised in North Dakota by a family who loved to share stories through food, Anne has always been interested in the history within the meals we share and the ways people grow food across cultures. A determined gardener, she's grown food and flowers wherever she could—rooftops, neighbors' yards, and community gardens. Today, she has a small cut flower farm on Lummi Island, where she lives with her partner, her dog, and a few hives of bees.

Kristen den Hartog is a writer whose love of gardening was inspired by her grandfather, a market gardener in the Netherlands. His World War II story is recounted in *The Occupied Garden*, which Kristen wrote with her sister, Tracy Kasaboski. The sisters' latest book is *The Cowkeeper's Wish*, which explores their maternal line through Victorian England and World War I. Kristen lives in Toronto, Canada.

Composed by North Market Street Graphics,
Lancaster, Pennsylvania

❀

Designed by Cindy Szili

❀

Printed and bound by LithtexNW,
Bellingham, Washington

Notes

Notes

Notes